MURDER OF INNOCENCE

For a complete list of books, visit JamesPatterson.com.

MURDER OF INNOCENCE

TRUE-CRIME THRILLERS

JAMES PATTERSON

As Seen on

**INVESTIGATION
DISCOVERY**

GRAND CENTRAL
PUBLISHING

NEW YORK   BOSTON

Grand Central Publishing
Hachette Book Group
1290 Avenue of the Americas, New York, NY 10104
grandcentralpublishing.com
twitter.com/grandcentralpub

First Edition: November 2020

Grand Central Publishing is a division of Hachette Book Group, Inc. The Grand Central name and logo are trademarks of Hachette Book Group, Inc.

The publisher is not responsible for websites (or their content) that are not owned by the publisher.

The Hachette Speakers Bureau provides a wide range of authors for speaking events. To find out more, go to hachettespeakersbureau.com or call (866) 376-6591.

ISBN 978-1-5387-5244-9 (paperback) / 978-1-5387-5245-6 (hardcover, library edition) / 978-1-5387-1903-9 (large print)
LCCN 2020935744

10 9 8 7 6 5 4 3 2 1

LSC-C

Printed in the United States of America

CONTENTS

MURDER OF INNOCENCE
(James Patterson with Max DiLallo)   1

A MURDEROUS AFFAIR
(James Patterson with Andrew Bourelle)   145

MURDER OF INNOCENCE

JAMES PATTERSON

WITH MAX DILALLO

PROLOGUE

July 14, 2000

CAREY FLUTTERS OPEN HER eyes, but she can't see much of anything.

Hot water is running down her face. Swirls of rising steam engulf her.

Her head is spinning, and her legs and arms feel wobbly, like the Jell-O shots she and her sorority sisters make for their house parties.

Carey has been drunk before. And stoned. More times than she can count.

But this feeling, what's happening to her right now, is different.

Very different.

Carey gropes blindly for something to hold on to. Her fingertips make contact with a wall of wet tile. She claws at the slick surface, feeling dangerously shaky. Then she forces herself to take some slow, deep breaths. And think.

She's standing upright in a hot shower. That much Carey's sure about.

But she has no idea *whose* shower.

Or where she is.

Or how in the hell she got here.

And—*oh God*—Carey realizes now that she's completely naked.

What happened to her clothes?

The last thing she remembers is the start of the night. It was Friday, and she and some girlfriends decided to head off campus and go barhopping on State Street, Santa Barbara's main drag. They ended up at O'Malley's, a popular, proudly inauthentic Irish pub. The place was packed with fellow University of California students, all drunk and sweaty, sloshing their Coors Lights and moving their bodies to pulsing hip-hop.

Most of the guys there were undergrads like Carey. But one of them was older. Quite a bit older. It was hard to tell for sure in the dim bar, but he looked well into his thirties. He seemed out of place in this sea of students, but he was tall, with a great head of dark hair, and he had a charm and confidence about him that most boys Carey's own age lacked. *Their* idea of flirting was leering at a girl, dropping a cheesy pickup line, then offering to buy her a couple of shots.

Not this man. He came up to her with a glass of ice

water from the bar already in hand—cold and refreshing, exactly what Carey was craving after hours on the dance floor—and struck up an actual conversation.

He introduced himself as Andrew. He asked what she was studying and where she was from. Art history and Sacramento, she told him. He said he'd grown up in California too. In Malibu and Brentwood, to be specific, which she knew were wealthy enclaves of nearby Los Angeles. He was a filmmaker. He loved to surf. He owned a bungalow on the beach in Mussel Shoals, a twenty-minute drive away. And he claimed he knew a secret recipe for the best margaritas in the entire world. Would Carey like to come over and have some?

That's where her memory begins to blur.

Which is why Carey deduces with horror that *she has been drugged.*

She can recall the rest of the night only in vague, dreamlike snippets. She remembers stumbling into the front seat of the man's forest green SUV. She remembers gripping his shoulder for support as she tottered along the beach behind his house. She remembers collapsing, loopy and exhausted, onto his couch.

But how did she end up in the shower?

Her breathing quickens as she tries to formulate a plan. If she can just stop her head from spinning, if she can just make her muscles work again, she can step out of the shower. She can get dressed. She can go home.

But Carey doesn't get the chance.

The bathroom door opens, and in walks the man from the bar.

He strips off his white linen shirt and board shorts, pulls back the shower curtain, and steps in behind Carey, brushing his nude body up against hers.

Carey gasps. She's filled with nausea and fear. She goes rigid from head to toe.

"Feels good, hmm?" he says, nuzzling Carey's neck and sliding his hands along her thighs and up to her bare breasts.

No, it doesn't feel good, Carey thinks. *Stop, please. No. Stop!*

Carey wants to scream and yell but no words come out, only muffled sobs.

She wants to fight off this monster. Spin around, knee this son of a bitch in the groin, dig her nails into his eyeballs.

But she just stands there in the running water. Frozen. Dazed. Helpless to speak up or resist.

Praying for this nightmare to end as the man pushes himself inside her.

CHAPTER 1

Four Years Earlier

PADDLE FASTER, DUDE, YOU'RE gonna miss it!"

Andrew Luster, still boyishly handsome at thirty-two, lies stomach-down on an eight-foot-long freshly waxed pinewood surfboard that glistens in the rising California sun. His arms are churning the water like a pair of twin-engine propellers.

Behind him, a massive wave is surging—and he's determined to catch it.

Heeding his friend's words, Andrew pumps his arms harder. A salty sea mist stings his eyes. His shoulders start to burn. But he doesn't let up. He's set his sights on that wave, and he'll be damned if he's going to let it get away.

That's the kind of man Andrew Luster is and always has been.

He's a man who knows exactly what he wants.

A man used to *getting* exactly what he wants.

No matter the cost.

Soon, the wave begins to swell. Andrew leaps up onto his board in a squatting position. As the water crests, he stands upright, turns sideways, and feels himself picking up speed.

"Yeah!" he shouts. He pumps his fist, savoring the thrill. "Hell yeah!"

But Andrew's joy is short-lived. Without warning, his board jerks. He loses his balance and belly-flops into the surf.

He quickly fights his way back to the surface, coughs up seawater. His friend Jon Balden—his neighbor and occasional early-morning surfing partner—is floating on his own board nearby, pointing at him and cackling. "Nice wipeout!"

For a moment, Andrew is overcome by a rush of shame and fury. He hates being laughed at almost as much as he hates not getting his way.

But then Andrew forces a smile, reverting to his typical, easygoing self. "I meant to do that!" he calls to Jon. "I just wish I'd gotten it on tape!"

He's only half joking. As much as he loves his surfboard, Andrew loves another toy even more: his Super VHS camcorder. His video camera is practically attached to his shoulder whenever he's not in the water. He films snippets of his daily life, documents his travels, interviews his friends. *Constantly.* He especially likes turning the camera on himself. Some might call this habit odd. Eccentric. Narcissistic. Andrew calls it his passion.

Andrew spins his surfboard around and is preparing to head back out when he sees his companion paddling toward the shore. "Come on! You're not quitting on me already, are you, Jon?"

"Wish I could stay out longer. But I've got somewhere to be this morning. It's called a job. *J-o-b*. Ever heard of it? You go to an office, sit at a desk, earn a salary? You should try it someday."

Andrew rolls his eyes. This isn't the first time his friend has teased him about his enviable lifestyle. One of the great-grandsons of Maksymilian Faktorowicz—better known as Max Factor Sr., founder of the mega-successful global cosmetics company that bears his name—Andrew was born into a life of incredible wealth and privilege. When Andrew turned eighteen, he was given access to a hefty trust fund, a portion of which he used to buy a cozy oceanside bungalow in the sleepy California beach town of Mussel Shoals.

That was almost fifteen years ago. He hasn't worked a single day since.

"Yeah, yeah," Andrew says, brushing off Jon's dig. "I'll probably hit the waves again later, around sunset, before I head downtown. You should join me. For both."

Jon shakes his head good-naturedly, well aware that when his neighbor says "downtown," he means the strip of bars he likes to haunt in nearby Santa Barbara.

College bars.

Women, the younger the better, are Andrew's third great passion in life. If he's not surfing or shooting home movies, he's talking about girls. Or chasing them. Or bedding them. Fit, tan, charming, and rich, Andrew has no trouble bringing home a different beautiful girl practically every night of the week. He rarely sees any of them twice.

"Sounds tempting, but maybe another time," Jon says. "I've got to go to work *tomorrow* morning too. Imagine that."

The men say goodbye and head their separate ways— Jon toward the shore, Andrew toward the waves.

As he scans the shimmering water looking for the next big swell, Andrew can't get Jon's mocking comments out of his head. So what if he doesn't work a traditional nine-to-five? So what if he was born wealthy? He gets to spend his days and nights doing what he loves.

Which suddenly gives Andrew an idea.

CHAPTER 2

AND...ACTION!"

On cue, three tall, voluptuous, gorgeous young women—a blonde, a brunette, and a redhead, each carrying a surfboard and each wearing a string bikini about the size of three postage stamps—begin jogging down the beach in front of Andrew's bungalow. They playfully push and swat one another, giggling.

Kneeling in the sand nearby is Andrew Luster. His bulky camcorder is perched on his shoulder; a dopey smile is plastered across his face. Peering through the viewfinder, he tracks the models as they run, filming every sultry second of it.

When they reach the water's edge, he yells, "Now get rid of those tops, girls! Let 'em fly!"

The trio fling their bikini tops into the air, pounce on their surfboards, leap into the shallows, and start paddling away. Water splashes all over their bronzed backs and shapely behinds.

"And . . . cut! That was great, ladies. Really great. Let's try it one more time."

A few hundred yards away, Jon Balden is cooking oatmeal in his kitchen; after he eats, he'll head to the office. Through the window, he notices what's happening on the beach. It's not uncommon to see pretty girls frolicking in the surf. But three statuesque models emerging from the water half naked while his neighbor *films* them?

Jon turns off the burner. He has to check this out for himself.

Jon starts marching down to the shore, where Andrew is standing in a huddle with the three women as they casually retie their bikini tops. He's giving them direction, pointing out where along the beach he wants them to scurry next.

"Quite the production you've got here, Mr. Spielberg," Jon calls out as he approaches. He means it as a joke, but that seems lost on Andrew, who beams with pride.

"I know, right? I'm a director now! Can you believe it?"

No, Jon thinks, *I can't.* "What are you shooting exactly? A homemade *Baywatch* porno parody?"

Now Andrew's smile starts to falter. He puts an arm around Jon's shoulders and guides him out of earshot of the talent. "You think this is porn? No way. This is a real Hollywood movie. I wrote the script myself. It's a surfing action comedy called *Waves and Babes*. It's gonna be huge."

Jon looks at his wacky neighbor for a moment, then lets out a belly laugh.

Andrew pouts, insulted.

Too late, Jon realizes Andrew was being completely serious. "I mean, uh...that's cool," Jon says, backpedaling.

"I started a real Hollywood production company too! Check this out."

Andrew excitedly reaches into the back pocket of his sandy board shorts, pulls out a stack of crumpled business cards, and hands one to Jon. The smudged lettering reads DEEP SIX FILMS ~ ANDREW S. LUSTER, PRESIDENT AND CEO.

Jon is at a loss for words. Is his friend delusional? He finally says, a little awkwardly, "That's great, Andrew. I'm excited for you."

Now it's Andrew's turn to laugh—smugly. "Thanks, bro. I'd love to keep chatting, but I've got to get back to *my job*."

Jon watches his surfing buddy return to his three scantily clad starlets. Andrew yells "Places!" then "Action!" and resumes filming them as they run and jiggle, strip off their bikini tops, and splash around in the water.

A real Hollywood movie? Yeah, right, Jon thinks.

All he knows for sure is that his neighbor is a real odd duck.

CHAPTER 3

TONJA STEPS OUT OF the terminal at Santa Barbara Airport and sets her bags down on the curb. She closes her eyes, enjoying the warm afternoon sunshine on her face. She exhales, savoring the delightful peace and quiet.

Compared to sprawling and chaotic Phoenix Sky Harbor International, where she departed from two hours ago, this tiny regional airport feels calm, even soothing. The single-story terminal building is made of smooth white stone, topped with a red-tile roof, and surrounded by swaying palm trees.

Tonja's big sister, Lisa, who had been begging her to come visit ever since she'd moved out here a few years ago, always said Santa Barbara was a little slice of paradise. Tonja's already starting to understand. *If the airport is this nice,* she thinks, *how gorgeous must the rest of this place be?*

Beep-beep. A gray Honda with a dented front bumper pulls up to the curb. Lisa hops out and throws her arms around her baby sister, then takes a step back and gives Tonja a once-over. Her eyes travel from Tonja's scuffed-up cowboy boots to her full denim skirt to her giant strawberry-blond perm. Lisa teasingly clicks her tongue. "You can take the girl out of Arizona, but you can't take the Arizona out of the girl."

Tonja feigns offense. "What's that supposed to mean?"

"You're in Southern California now, not the Wild West. But don't worry. I've got the perfect dress for you to borrow. You're going to look amazing in it."

"I think I look fine in *this* outfit, thank you very much."

"Of course you do. But that's not the point. You're skinny, you're gorgeous, and you're twenty-one. You'd look hot wearing a garbage bag."

"Is that supposed to be a compliment?"

Lisa laughs. "Come on. Toss your crap in the trunk and let's go."

The ride from the airport to Lisa's place is short and dazzlingly scenic. They pass sweeping hillsides, gorgeous Spanish mission–style mansions, stunning views of the glimmering Pacific. Tonja's jaw hangs open the entire time.

Lisa's apartment isn't nearly as grand; it's a modest one-bedroom rental in a middle-class part of town. But it's bright and breezy and clean and just a few minutes' drive from both the beach and downtown.

Tonja flops onto her sister's pullout couch, where she'll be spending the next five nights. Her trip has barely begun and already she's feeling sad about leaving.

"Here's that dress I was talking about," Lisa says. She emerges from her room holding up what is essentially a wisp of fabric, magenta with a white floral print. "What do you think?"

"That's a *dress?* I have headbands bigger than that."

"That's your problem. Just try it on."

"Maybe later. I was thinking tonight we'd slip into some pj's, order a pizza, watch some trashy TV, and just talk. Like we used to do when we were kids."

"Are you joking? This is your first night in Santa Barbara," Lisa says, tossing the slinky outfit at Tonja. "We're going out!"

A few hours later, all dressed up, their hair done, in full makeup, the two sisters hit the town. They start the evening by grabbing some grilled fish tacos at a fantastic hole-in-the-wall Mexican place Lisa knows and washing them down with ice-cold Tecate beers. Next they head to State Street, a glitzy strip of bars and restaurants stretching from the beach to the foot-hills. Even though it's a weeknight, the area is teeming with people, a mix of well-heeled tourists, local beach bums, and rowdy college students. Tonja soaks up all the sights and sounds, loving every moment.

The sisters go to a few different spots, downing a drink at each. Eventually they find themselves at Calypso, a combination grill and nightclub with a kitschy tropical theme. They're on the dance floor together, grooving blissfully to some reggaeton, when Tonja feels a tap on her shoulder.

"Hey, I love your dress."

Tonja turns to see a tall, good-looking man. His brown hair is thick and wavy. His shoulders are broad. But he's in his thirties, a decade older than the guys she's usually attracted to.

Normally Tonja's first instinct would be to brush him off. Even if he were her own age, she's here to hang out with her sister, not to let unknown men hit on her. Yet there's something striking about this one, something undeniably alluring. An instant spark.

So Tonja says, "Thank you," and unconsciously tugs the hemline of her tight magenta skirt down toward her knees, bashful under his gaze.

"You look a little thirsty," the man says. He flashes Tonja a smile—warm, friendly, instantly disarming. "Here. Do you want a glass of water?"

CHAPTER 4

NO, THANKS," LISA SAYS, butting in. "But we'd *love* a couple of vodka and cranberries."

The man pauses for a moment, then bobs his head. "What do you say we grab a table on the patio?" he asks. "It's quieter out there. Easier to have a real conversation."

"Sounds like a plan," Lisa answers, and the man heads toward the bar.

"What are you *doing?*" Tonja demands. "Do you even know that guy?"

Lisa shakes her head. "But I saw the way you were looking at him." Tonja blushes. "I think he's kinda cute too! Look, let's just sit down for a minute, give our feet a rest, have a free drink, make a little small talk, then we'll leave. What do you say?"

Tonja isn't thrilled about the idea of leading a guy on like this, but she agrees.

A few minutes later, Tonja, Lisa, and the man are

easing onto a banquette on the rear patio. Flickering
tiki torches cast shadows across their faces.

"Three Grey Gooses and cranberry," he announces.
He hands Tonja and Lisa each a glass filled with ruby-
red liquid and keeps one for himself. "Cheers. To new
friends. And new adventures."

They all clink glasses and take a sip. The sharp tang
of alcohol catches Tonja by surprise. "Wow," she says.
"These are pretty strong."

"Mike, the bartender—he's a friend of mine. I asked
him to mix them like that."

Lisa introduces herself and her little sister, Tonja.
"She's visiting from Arizona," Lisa tells him.

"No kidding," the man says, turning and staring intently into Tonja's eyes. "I would've guessed you came
from heaven."

Lisa groans. It's a painfully corny line, and all three
of them know it. But Tonja genuinely laughs. Maybe
it's the booze. Maybe it's his magnetism. Or maybe it's
something else.

"I'm Andrew, by the way. And I couldn't be happier
to meet you both."

From there, the conversation flows easily. Despite
his cheesy intro, Andrew is suave and engaging. He
drops enticing hints about his life, which sounds quite
charmed. He tells the two women that he's a successful
screenwriter and director and that he owns a major
production company.

"Would we have seen any of your movies?" Lisa asks.

"Probably not. I've been focusing on smaller, independent films so far."

When Tonja says she's considering a career in real estate, Andrew shares his experience buying his beachside bungalow and offers some thoughts on the Southern California property market. When she says she's always wanted to try surfing, Andrew practically leaps out of his seat. He'd love to teach her sometime.

"Another drink?" he asks Tonja as she's finishing the last sip of her cocktail.

It's Lisa who answers. "Thanks, but it's getting late. We should probably—"

"Sure!" Tonja interjects.

Andrew holds up his hand and gets the attention of a passing waiter, who hurries right over. "Hey, Andrew, good to see you! What can I get you guys?"

"Brian, these are my new friends, the lovely Tonja and her equally lovely sister, Lisa. We'd like another round, please."

Andrew removes a massive wad of folded cash from his pocket and slips a bill into the waiter's palm. It's dark on the patio, but Tonja sees it's a hundred. The waiter nods appreciatively and scurries off.

"The bartender, the servers—seems like you're pretty popular around here," Lisa says.

If Andrew detects a hint of judgment in her voice, he ignores it. "That's because I *love* it here. I work hard, I play hard." Subtly brushing his fingertips across Tonja's forearm, he adds, "Is that a crime?"

The next round of drinks arrives and the conversation continues.

Tonja can tell that Lisa is unimpressed by Andrew. Rich LA guy, full of himself, likes to party and hit on younger women. Thinks he's a total bad boy but is about as exciting—and dangerous—as a wet beach towel. Living in Santa Barbara, Lisa has met his type a million times, and that's what she tells her little sister under her breath while Andrew's busy chatting to another waiter.

Tonja shrugs off Lisa's comment. She's hanging on Andrew's every word. She's flattered by his attention, charmed by his confidence, and more impressed by his money and success than she wants to admit to herself. When she finishes her second drink, she's the one who suggests a third.

"Now it's *really* getting late," Lisa says with a sigh. "Tonja, you're probably wiped out from traveling. It was nice meeting you, Andrew, but we should get going."

"Actually, I feel great!" Tonja says brightly. "You can leave if you want. I'll take a cab back or something."

Lisa gives her younger sister a long, hard look. Is this really what she wants? Tonja stares back steadily. She's an adult, old enough to make her own decisions, live her own life.

"Okay. Sure," Lisa finally says. "You two have fun. I'll see you when you get home, Ton."

Alone with Andrew on the banquette, Tonja scoots a little closer to him. "Should we order more drinks?" she asks.

Andrew grins. Rests a hand on her bare knee.

"I was thinking...I could *make* us some. Back at my place. I know a secret recipe for the best margaritas in the world."

CHAPTER 5

ANDREW PULLS HIS FOREST GREEN SUV into his driveway. He cuts the engine, which starts ticking like a metronome as it cools. He walks around the car, opens Tonja's door, takes her hand, and helps her climb out.

"Such a gentleman," she says with a coy smile.

It's a chivalrous move, certainly. But it's also a necessary one. After a long night of drinking, Tonja's a little unsteady on her feet.

Andrew guides his guest up the path to his home. Tonja's arm is slung around his shoulders. Andrew's is wrapped low around her slender waist. "Welcome to Villa Luster," he jokes when they reach his front door.

As he unlocks it and lets them in, Tonja gives the outside of the bungalow a long look. A villa? Not even close. The place looks quaint and inviting, but it's much more modest than she was expecting based on

Andrew's boasts of wealth and success. Then again, he *had* seemed like the kind of guy who values things like traveling and experiences over material possessions. Maybe his home simply reflects that. Tonja keeps these thoughts to herself.

Andrew flips on the lights to reveal a clean, cozy quintessential bachelor pad, confirming Tonja's theory. In the living room, a well-worn beige sofa faces a massive TV that's hooked up to three professional-looking VCRs. In the dining room, there are half a dozen colorful wooden surfboards stacked in a corner. In the kitchen, a few empty takeout containers rest on the counter. There isn't much furniture, and hardly anything is hung on the walls. Andrew might be in his thirties, but his home looks like a college dorm room.

"Sit, sit, please," Andrew says, gesturing theatrically toward his couch. "I'll make us some delectable frozen libations."

Tonja giggles and flops onto the sofa. Andrew walks into the adjoining kitchen and starts dumping ice cubes from a plastic tray into an old blender.

"Do you want to call your sister, tell her where you are? Phone's over there."

Tonja waves her hand as if swatting an invisible fly. "What for? She's probably fast asleep by now anyway."

Andrew uncaps a bottle of Jose Cuervo Especial Silver tequila and pours a few good glugs into the blender. Then a few more. "You two seem pretty close. But also pretty different."

"You've got that right," Tonja says, looking around the place. "Lisa's always been the 'good' daughter. Studious, hardworking, dependable. Finished college. Steady job. Long-term boyfriends. All that stuff. She's a total straight-edge too."

"What do you mean?"

Tonja glances back at Andrew in the kitchen. He's pouring something blue that resembles antifreeze into the blender. "Is that Kool-Aid?"

"Hey, no peeking! This is my secret recipe!"

Tonja laughs and covers her eyes. She starts to apologize, but her words are drowned out by the deafening roar of the blender; it's so loud, it practically shakes the bungalow walls. Moments later, Andrew joins her on the couch with two tall glasses filled with a frosty, aquamarine slush.

"Blue curaçao," he announces. "*That's* the secret ingredient. Promise you won't tell a soul?"

"Cross my heart." Tonja takes a sip of her drink, then smacks her lips in delight. "So good!" she blurts out. "I thought it would taste like blueberry, but it's orange."

Andrew gives her a sly smile. "With me, things aren't always what they seem." Then he says, "You never answered my question before. You called your sister a 'total straight-edge.' What did you mean by that?"

"I just meant she's not a big partier. She'll have a few drinks now and then, like tonight, but that's it."

"What about you?"

Tonja thinks for a moment before answering. "The way I look at it, life is short. I want to live as much as I can. Have as much fun as I can. Try as many things as I can."

Now it's Andrew who pauses before asking, slowly, "What about . . . GHB?"

Tonja squints in confusion. "I don't think I know what that is."

"You never heard of liquid X? Just a couple of drops, and you'll feel like you're floating on a cloud. It's tasteless, odorless, and totally harmless. Want to try some?"

Tonja feels a shiver of excitement run down her spine. Of course she knows it's risky to try a new drug, especially with a guy she barely knows. But that's part of what makes the idea so tempting. "Okay," she says with a mischievous smile. "But just a little."

"You're gonna love it!" Andrew claps his hands in excitement, then pulls a tiny glass vial from the inner pocket of his jeans. Inside is a clear liquid.

He unscrews the cap and holds the vial over Tonja's blue drink.

"I lied," Andrew says. "My margarita recipe? *This* is the secret ingredient."

CHAPTER 6

TONJA FLUTTERS OPEN HER eyes, but she can't see much of anything.

She's blinded by a warm ray of sunlight streaming in through an open window. Outside, she hears the soothing lap of waves against the sand and the cawing of a distant flock of seagulls.

Tonja rolls over. Rubs her aching temples. Looks around.

She's in an empty, unfamiliar bedroom, lying on top of the covers in an empty, unfamiliar bed.

Her head feels heavy, her mind hazy; it's like having a bad hangover mixed with a sinus infection. Slowly she starts to get her bearings and piece together where she is.

This must be Andrew's room, she thinks. But he's nowhere to be seen.

And she has no memory of how she got here.

Worse, Tonja realizes that after Andrew gave her that GHB-laced margarita last night, she has no memory of what happened *at all.*

With dread, she glances down—and is pleasantly surprised to see that she's fully clothed. The magenta-and-white floral-print dress she borrowed from Lisa is rumpled, but just barely. Her bra, nylons, and under-wear are all still in place as well. Even the strappy sandals she wore last night are still on her feet.

Tonja exhales, deeply relieved. She was very much attracted to Andrew and was having a great time getting to know him. But she definitely wasn't ready to sleep with him yet. Certainly not under the influence of a strange new drug.

Now Tonja likes him even more. As she knows from stories she's heard, plenty of guys in his position might have pushed her to do things she wasn't comfortable with. Others might have taken advantage of her in her altered state.

But not Andrew.

Tonja is starting to think that maybe, just maybe, after years of dating creeps and jerks, she's finally found a real gentleman.

The bedroom door opens. "Great, you're awake!" Andrew bounds into the room. He's carrying a steaming mug of coffee and a plate with a mound of scrambled eggs and two pieces of whole-wheat toast. He looks like he's just returned from surfing; his hair is messy and damp, and he smells faintly of the ocean.

"What a night, huh?" he chirps. "How are you feeling?"

Tonja adjusts herself so she's sitting up in bed. "Okay, I guess," she answers, her voice scratchy and hoarse. "Tired. A little groggy."

"Totally. I felt the same way the first couple of times I did liquid X. You'll get used to it. Here." He thrusts the mug and plate at her. "A cup of joe and a hearty breakfast. This should have you feeling like new in no time."

Tonja thanks him for the coffee and food but then says, tentatively, "Andrew, after we took that GHB last night, I don't remember a thing. What happened? How did I end up in your bed?"

Andrew chuckles and drapes a friendly arm across Tonja's shoulders. "Of course you don't remember a thing—you passed out about thirty seconds after your first sip! So I carried you into the bedroom and laid you down on the bed."

Tonja looks over at the unwrinkled patch of gray duvet cover beside her. "Did you sleep here too?"

"Of course not. I slept on the couch."

Tonja feels her cheeks grow a few shades rosier as she asks softly, "So I guess that means, you know...nothing *happened* between us?"

Andrew makes a face as if that were the silliest question in the world. "You think I would—no way!" He lowers himself onto the bed beside Tonja. "Look...I know you're in California for only a few more days. But I had a great time last night. I'd really love to see you again."

Tonja feels her stomach fill with butterflies. Andrew's words bring her so much joy, she can barely contain it. "Me too. You must be really busy running your production company—"

Andrew cuts her off and asks with a giant smile, "Are you free tonight?"

CHAPTER 7

TOWER, CESSNA THREE-THREE-SIX Victor Bravo at runway one-zero. Ready for takeoff, over."

"Roger, Cessna three-three-six, you are clear to fly."

Tonja is giddy with excitement as she hears the voices crackle in her headset.

Andrew is sitting beside her. He's also wearing a headset—and holding his bulky video camera on his shoulder. With his free arm, he pulls Tonja's trembling body close and gives her a comforting squeeze.

The two are already pressed tightly together in the second row of this tiny prop plane. Up front sits Garrett, their pilot for the afternoon.

Tonja lets out a little gasp as Garrett engages the throttle and the plane rockets forward. It starts to pick up even more speed, rumbling and shuddering down the runway. At last, Garrett eases back on the yoke and...liftoff.

Tonja stares out the window in silent awe as the plane climbs higher and higher into the blue sky. Below, the hilly green and brown landscape of greater Santa Barbara rapidly falls away.

Tonja has been on plenty of commercial flights before, but she's never experienced the thrill of anything quite like this.

"Pretty quiet back there," Garrett says from the cockpit. "You two all right?"

Tonja's eyes are still glued to the scene out the window. Andrew's, through his camera's viewfinder, are on Tonja.

"Doing great," Andrew answers. "Just admiring . . . *the beauty.*"

Tonja turns and blushes at Andrew's comment. She plants an affectionate kiss on his lips—one of many they've shared over the whirlwind of the past few days.

Since the night they met, the two have hardly left each other's sides. Andrew has taken Tonja on a string of romantic dates, each more lavish than the last. He's treated her to fancy dinners, gifted her a shopping spree at a high-end clothing boutique in nearby Montecito, whisked her to a wine-tasting in the foothills of Santa Ynez, and, of course, given her a surfing lesson in the waves behind his home. He's even introduced her to some of his friends, like his neighbor Jon.

But a private ride in a prop plane?

Tonja thought Andrew was joking when he told her

his idea. She couldn't believe it; it seemed too extreme, too extravagant, even for a man as wealthy as him.

A man she's known for less than a week.

Tonja has dated guys who tried to sweep her off her feet. But none of them were this successful. And none of them did it, well, *literally*.

The flight lasts for an entire magical hour, and Andrew films every minute of it as Garrett takes them zigzagging through the clouds above Santa Barbara County, then into the neighboring county of Ventura.

"I think that's my house!" Andrew jokes, pointing down at the scenic shoreline.

Tonja laughs and gives him a playful tap. Viewed from this height, the homes are totally indistinguishable, just orange-roofed little boxes nestled between the lush hills and the endless expanse of deep blue ocean.

After looping back over the water and passing above the rocky Channel Islands just off the coast, Garrett brings them in for a smooth landing at Santa Barbara Airport.

Tonja can't help but marvel at her incredible good fortune. When she landed at this same airport just days ago, she'd expected a relaxing visit with her older sister. Now here she is in a private plane with a charming, rich, wonderful man. It's all beyond her wildest dreams.

But then an upsetting thought crosses Tonja's mind.

She tries to push her concerns away as they exit the plane, tries to keep a big smile on her face as Andrew films her strutting across the tarmac. Too bad Tonja's a terrible actress. Andrew can instantly tell something's bothering her. He shuts off the camera and asks what's wrong. Did she not enjoy the flight?

Tonja sniffles, her eyes damp. "No, of course not, I loved it. It's just that...two days from now, I'll be catching *another* flight. Back to Arizona. And I don't want to go. I wish I didn't have to. Because...I think I'm falling in love with you, Andrew."

Andrew is nearly as overcome as Tonja. "I don't *think* I'm falling in love with you, Tonja. I *know* I am."

"You are? Really? Then...what are we going to do?"

Andrew gently thumbs away a tear that has rolled down Tonja's cheek. "Let's go home. Talk about it. And do some more liquid X to help us think."

CHAPTER 8

WITH SATISFIED GRUNTS, Andrew Luster and his neighbor Jon Balden set a heavy cardboard box labeled SHOES down on Andrew's living-room floor.

About a dozen other boxes are already there, each with a label — CLOTHES, FRAGILE, KITCHEN — written in black Sharpie in Tonja's looping cursive.

"Is that the last of 'em?" Andrew asks.

Tonja and Lisa have just come in carrying a few old shopping bags full of toiletries, books, and various odds and ends.

"Almost," Tonja answers. "I think one more trip should do it."

"Great! Give me two seconds, guys. I'll meet you out there."

Tonja, Jon, and Lisa head back outside into the cool evening air. Parked in Andrew's driveway next to his green SUV is a rented U-Haul moving van. After nine hours of rattling across the dusty desert highways of Arizona and California, the van is speckled the color of cinnamon.

"Thanks again for helping us out, Jon," Tonja says. "I really appreciate it."

"Hey, no problem. That's what neighbors are for. And as of today, you're officially my neighbor."

The three step up into the rear of the truck. It's empty except for a few small tote bags and one cardboard box labeled MISC.

"To be honest, I still don't think it's hit me yet," Tonja says. "That this beautiful, incredible place is going to be my new home."

"It'll take a while," Lisa says, "but eventually, that feeling will wear off."

"Speak for yourself," Jon says. "I've lived around here my whole life, and some days, I still have to pinch myself."

Tonja reaches for one of the tote bags, then stops. A wave of self-doubt is suddenly washing over her. "You both think I'm crazy, don't you? Quitting my job. Uprooting my entire life. Moving in with a guy I've known for about three weeks."

Lisa smirks. "Jon, you answer this one. Tonja knows how *I* feel about it."

"Okay. I think it's great. It's a big leap, sure, but it's obvious Andrew's nuts about you. Hell, I think this is the longest relationship he's had in years!" Jon chuckles.

Lisa rolls her eyes, but Tonja stiffens. "Are you serious?" Has Andrew really never had a long-term girlfriend before?

"I'm joking!" Jon says. "Come on, let's finish this up."

Tonja and Lisa collect the tote bags. Jon bends down to lift the box.

"Wait, wait! I need to get this on tape!"

Andrew has emerged from the house with his camcorder nestled on his shoulder, its little RECORD light twinkling like a red star.

"How about you put down the camera and help me carry this," Jon says.

"I just want a few seconds," Andrew insists. "This is such a special day. I want to remember it forever. Now, big smiles, all of you. And...action!"

Grudgingly, Tonja, Lisa, and Jon let Andrew film them carrying the final items off the truck and into his beach house. He follows them inside, then zooms in for a close-up of Tonja as she turns around. "Anything you want to say for the camera, beautiful?"

Tonja lets out a nervous but adorable laugh. "Uh...just that...I'm really, really happy. I feel like the luckiest girl in the world."

Some two hours later, Andrew and Tonja are alone, cuddled up together on the sofa, bellies full of Chinese takeout and chardonnay.

"I'm so glad you said yes when I asked you to move in, baby." Andrew puts his arm around Tonja and nuzzles her neck. "I wasn't sure you would. But we're gonna have such a good life together."

Tonja couldn't agree more. She shuts her eyes and moans with pleasure.

Soon Andrew's lips find their way to hers. They start to kiss. Tenderly at first, then with growing passion.

"Let's move this to the bedroom," Tonja whispers, adding with a sexy smile, "I want to show you just how good a roommate I'm going to be."

Andrew nods, but then says, "I was thinking...maybe tonight we could try something...a little different."

"Like what?"

He gestures to his video camera resting on a nearby cardboard box. "Make a little movie. Of us. Know what I'm saying?"

Tonja hesitates; the idea makes her all kinds of uncomfortable. "Um, I don't know. I'm nervous. I've never done anything like that before."

"So? You'd never tried liquid X before either, right? Come on. Don't be so uptight. It's gonna be really hot. Trust me."

Tonja bites her lip. She does trust Andrew. And she doesn't want to be a wet blanket. Maybe she's making too big a deal out of it?

Finally, as a compromise, she offers to take off some of her clothes on camera. "But you have to promise you'll *never* show the tape to anyone."

"Cross my heart, baby. Hope to die."

CHAPTER 9

IT FEELS LIKE A permanent vacation!"

That's how Tonja describes her first two months living with Andrew Luster in Mussel Shoals to anyone who asks. To her parents, back in Arizona. To Lisa, in nearby Santa Barbara. And especially to all the new friends she's been making at the gym, the salon, and in her real estate license class at UCSB.

Starting this new chapter of her life has turned out to be one of the best decisions Tonja has ever made. Any worries she might've had have faded away in the crisp, clean, ocean-scented California air.

So, too, have any doubts about moving in with a man she barely knew. In fact, her moving in has only made their relationship stronger. Andrew still dotes on her. Still takes her on expensive dates. Still whips up his "special" margaritas that send her to the moon.

Not that everything between them is perfect. There

are times Tonja wishes Andrew would open up to her more, share more about his past, his childhood, his previous relationships, instead of just shrugging or changing the subject.

And then there's that damn video camera of his. For the life of her, Tonja can't understand why Andrew insists on filming the two of them all the time. Taping their lovemaking is one thing. At least that's a little naughty. But recording them making *lunch?* Getting gas? Folding laundry? Tonja has learned to more or less ignore her boyfriend's strange hobby, but she wouldn't mind if he got a different one.

Tonja takes a deep breath, relishing the salty Pacific breeze. She digs her toes into the sand. She turns a page in the hefty real estate textbook resting on her thighs.

Andrew has gone out for the afternoon to run a few errands, so Tonja is using her time alone to sit outside and study. Reading about estoppel certificates and escrow accounts can be pretty dry, but reading about them on a gorgeous semiprivate beach makes it a whole lot better.

When she's finished studying, Tonja heads inside and pours herself a frosty glass of iced tea. Andrew should be home in about an hour. Feeling sluggish from the sun, she considers either taking a catnap or going for a refreshing dip in the ocean. In any case, she'll have to change out of her sandy sundress, so she heads for the bedroom.

That's when Tonja notices something...unusual.

There's a tiny storage closet in the hallway that's crammed with all manner of junk and doodads that Andrew has collected over the years. At least, that's what Tonja *thinks* is in there. She realizes now that, in the two months she's lived here, she hasn't once opened that closet; come to think of it, Tonja has never even seen the door open. Until now.

There it is, slightly ajar, the sliver of darkness on the other side beckoning her.

Tonja can't contain her curiosity. She pushes it open. And sees...

Just what she was expecting. The inside is filled with shelves and boxes of videotapes, clothing, knickknacks, papers, camera equipment. Tonja exhales, relieved.

She's about to shut the door when something catches her eye.

Pinned on the far wall is a giant collage of photographs. Of young women.

Tonja steps into the closet for a closer look.

There are dozens and dozens of pictures, each of a different pretty girl wearing a tight dress, bikini, or underwear. Each is laughing, waving, or smiling seductively. All are unfamiliar faces.

Tonja scans the photos. There's nothing wrong with them, exactly. All the women look to be of legal age, and none are in the nude.

But something about this discovery leaves Tonja unsettled.

She can't put her finger on it, but isn't it strange—creepy, even—that her boyfriend has this altar to the female form hidden away like this?

It gnaws at Tonja the rest of the afternoon and evening. When she and Andrew are getting ready for bed that night, she finally works up the nerve to bring it up.

"Babe...there's something I have to ask you. You know that storage closet in the hall? Well, earlier today, I looked inside and—"

"You did *what?* Why?"

"The door was open. I was curious. And, and...I saw all those pictures up on the wall. All those other girls. And I guess...I'm just wondering...who are they?"

Andrew glares at Tonja. He looks furious—but only for a moment. He quickly hides his flash of anger with an easy grin.

"They're just friends of mine, baby. Don't worry about it."

"Friends?"

"Yeah. Most of them are actresses. They want to be in my movies."

"But—"

"Didn't you hear me? Jesus, Tonja, I said don't worry about it. Okay?"

CHAPTER 10

DON'T WORRY ABOUT IT.

Those four little words have been echoing in Tonja's head all week.

And they're the exact opposite of what she's been doing.

Tonja hasn't been able to shake the image of the photo collage from her mind. Could all those beautiful half-naked women really just be Andrew's friends and aspiring actresses? If not, who are they? Exes? Objects of his affection?

And why did he get so mad when she asked him about it?

Honestly, that's what's troubling her the most. Tonja has always considered Andrew Luster a laid-back, easygoing guy. The only time he raises his voice is to yell "Action!" when he's filming. But that night, she got a glimpse of a whole other side of him. A nasty side. A scary side.

Which is why she's sitting in the lobby of an unfamiliar office building waiting to meet the one person who might be able to give her some answers.

"Tonja, hi! Sorry, a client meeting ran long."

She shoots to her feet as Jon approaches. Having only ever seen her neighbor wearing a grimy T-shirt and board shorts or a sand-covered wetsuit, she almost doesn't recognize Jon Balden in his pressed slacks and tie. "No worries," she answers. "You look nice, Jon."

"Thanks. You too. Shall we?"

Together they step out into the dry heat of midday. Jon leads them to a coffee shop nearby and insists on paying for whatever she wants. He orders a double espresso. Tonja asks for a bottle of chilled mineral water. The last thing she needs right now is caffeine. She's feeling jittery enough as it is.

"Thanks again for meeting me," she says as they take a seat in a cozy booth.

"Happy to," Jon answers. "Although, you know, anytime you want to chat, you can just walk the ten feet over to my place and knock." Jon smiles. But Tonja nervously rubs the lip of her water bottle.

"Yeah, but then Andrew might see. And I wanted to talk to you...alone."

Jon shifts in his seat. "Okay. What's up?"

After an awkwardly long pause, Tonja spills it. She tells Jon about the hidden photo collage, about Andrew's outburst, about her doubts, concerns, and fears.

"I know you're his friend. I would never want to put you in the middle of anything. But Andrew's so hard to talk to sometimes, you know? He's always so vague about his life before I met him. Am I getting worked up over nothing?"

Jon stares into his muddy cup of java, thinking hard.

"Back when he was single," he says, "sure, he did seem like a ladies' man. It wouldn't surprise me if he kept a couple pictures lying around of actresses he's worked with or some of his former flings. But so what? This is the same guy who keeps his video camera rolling twenty-four hours a day!"

They share a knowing laugh. Jon sips his coffee. Then he adds, "I always had a feeling it would take a very special girl to tame a guy like Andrew Luster. Not just beauty but brains. Kindness. A good heart. That's you, Tonja."

Jon reaches across the table and places a comforting hand on top of hers.

Tonja finds her eyes welling up—and she's flooded with relief. If Andrew has friends in his life as great as Jon, she figures he couldn't possibly be all that bad.

"Thank you, Jon. That . . . that means a lot to me."

CHAPTER 11

THE DIGITAL CLOCK ON Tonja's nightstand flashes 12:16 a.m. She's been lying in bed tossing and turning, unable to fall asleep, for over two hours.

Because Andrew is nowhere to be found.

Part of her is concerned about his safety. But mostly, she's angry.

At him and at herself.

This isn't the first time he's done this—gone out alone at night and been vague about where he was going, who he was seeing, and when he'd be home. Lisa told her it was a red flag, but Tonja didn't think much about it. At least, not the first few instances. She's Andrew's girlfriend, not his nanny. And besides, she has dinners and cocktails with girlfriends all the time without him. Why can't he go out once in a while without her?

But the past few months, it's been happening more and more often. And Andrew has been staying out later and later, coming home drunker and drunker. And increasingly, whenever Tonja presses him for details, he gets evasive—and dismissive.

Several worst-case scenarios run through Tonja's head. She hopes Andrew is just blowing off steam, but maybe he's cheating on her. Maybe he's losing interest in her. Maybe he has a secret family. Maybe he has a whole other secret life!

Tonja can't take it anymore; she needs something to calm her down. She flings off the covers, marches into the kitchen, grabs a glass tumbler and a bottle of Smirnoff. She pours a double shot, downs it in one go. Then she pours and downs another. She starts to pour a third but the glass slips from her hand and— *smash!*—shatters.

"Damn it, shit!" Tonja exclaims, then carefully tip-toes, barefoot, around the shards. She glances around the kitchen for a broom but doesn't see one. She looks under the sink for a dustpan. Nothing.

Then she gets an idea.

Tonja pads down the hall and opens the door to the storage closet. Sure enough, tucked in the back corner is a wooden outdoor broom, so old and unused that it has a cobweb across the bristles.

Tonja takes the broom and turns to go, but her eyes fall on that massive, creepy photo collage.

She hasn't looked at it since the day she discovered it, months ago. She hasn't wanted to. Tonight, when she's already upset with Andrew, the sight of it practically makes her sick. All those bright young faces smiling back at her, mocking her.

Then Tonja notices something else.

At the edge of the collage, Andrew has added a new picture.

A photograph of her.

Shocked, Tonja squints, leans forward, and examines the picture of herself with horror. In it, she's lying on a towel on the beach, waving happily at the camera, wearing a lime-green bikini.

Tonja can't remember the exact day the photo was taken. She often wears that bikini and frequently lies on the beach.

In fact, Tonja can't remember Andrew ever taking a photo of her. He's always shooting with his video camera, never a still-image camera. Tonja wonders if the photo is actually a freeze-frame of some tape. Maybe all of these are. Not that it matters.

Tonja feels violated and disgusted that Andrew has pinned her up on this wall of floozy actresses and past conquests. She rips her photo down and tears it into pieces, then storms back into the kitchen, tosses the shredded pieces into the trash, hastily sweeps up the broken glass, and dumps it on top.

By the time she's done, Tonja is even more riled up and breathing heavily. No way she'll ever get to sleep now.

But then she feels those two double shots of vodka creeping up on her.

She takes some slow, calming breaths and heads back to the bedroom. *Screw that bastard,* she thinks. *He doesn't deserve to have me wait up for him.* Tonja lies down and passes out within minutes.

She wakes with a start—groggy, disoriented—to the sound of Andrew yelling.

"How dare you! Who the hell do you think you are?"

He's standing at the foot of the bed, swaying from drunkenness, slurring his thunderous words.

Tonja quickly sits up, terrified. She's never seen her boyfriend act like this, never seen this venom in his glassy eyes.

"Andrew, calm down! What's wrong?"

"You...you took down your photo! Admit it, you bitch!"

Before Tonja can respond, Andrew lunges at her.

With both hands, he grasps the front of the tank top she's wearing and gives her a vigorous shake.

"Andrew, stop it! You're hurting me!"

But he only shakes her harder. "If you ever touch that again, I...I...I'll kill you!"

CHAPTER 12

WITH EXHAUSTED GRUNTS, TONJA and Jon Balden set a heavy trash bag bulging with shoes down on the floor of Tonja's new apartment.

It joins the mountains of other plastic garbage bags scattered around the drab, cramped, ground-floor studio Tonja has just rented a few miles up the coast from Andrew's place.

Unlike her last move, this one was rushed, disorganized, and urgent. Tonja couldn't stand living with Andrew Luster for one more minute.

"That does it," Lisa says, coming in and dropping a final bag on the scuffed linoleum floor of Tonja's kitchenette. She adds, softly but sharply, "Can't wait to do this all again in another four months."

Tonja turns to her sister, her face pinched with shame. "Shut up, Lisa."

"I tried to warn you, didn't I? I told you moving in with Andrew so fast was a—"

"How was I supposed to know he'd turn out to be a crazy lying maniac?"

"Come on, you two, don't fight," Jon says, playing peacemaker. "It's been a long day. We're all tired. The important thing is, Tonja's out of there now. For good."

Lisa sighs. "You're right. I'm sorry."

"I'm sorry too," Tonja says. "Thanks for all your help."

The sisters hug, long and tight. After Lisa leaves, Tonja locks the door behind her and engages the dead bolt. Then she turns to Jon.

And nearly breaks down.

"I'm so stupid! She did try to warn me, but I didn't listen. And now look at my life. It's a total disaster!"

"Hey," Jon says, rushing over and taking her in his arms. "Don't say that. You fell for Andrew's charms just like we all did. But now you're getting back on your feet. Plus, think of it this way—if none of this had happened, you probably never would have met *me*."

Tonja sniffles, hugs Jon closer, then tilts her head up and gives him a kiss.

The irony of their situation isn't lost on her—it took her moving in with a total madman to find real love with his wonderful neighbor.

But the danger isn't lost on her either.

After Andrew drunkenly threatened to kill her a few

weeks ago, his moods and behavior grew even more erratic. He started bullying Tonja and putting her down. He went out partying alone almost every night, often not coming home until the next day, then yelling and cursing at Tonja if she asked him where he'd been.

Tonja began seeking out Jon's advice—and company—more and more often. One evening, their friendship turned romantic.

When she was finally ready to leave Andrew and move out, Jon helped her find a new apartment and strategize how best to break things off—which actually went more smoothly than Tonja had thought it would.

Still, she and Jon have agreed it's best to keep their new relationship a secret for now. If Andrew found out they were dating, God only knows what he might do.

"Do you want to start unpacking things?" Jon asks. "Or leave it till tomorrow?"

"Tomorrow, definitely. All I want to do is take a hot shower and go to sleep."

"On the bare mattress?"

"Honestly, I could pass out on a bed of nails right now."

After taking a long, soothing shower, Tonja exits the bathroom—and gasps.

With delight.

Jon has surprised her by unpacking a set of sheets and pillows and making up her new bed. It's a small gesture, but to Tonja, it means so much. Jon might not have the chiseled jawline, the massive fortune, or the alluring bad-boy streak that Andrew does. But he's a kind and decent man, and Tonja feels deeply grateful to be with him.

She slips under the covers as Jon goes into the bathroom. Tonja's eyelids feel heavy; she could doze off any moment. But she wills herself to stay awake until her new boyfriend comes back. She doesn't want to fall asleep without giving him a good-night kiss.

Then Tonja hears a faint rustling in the bushes outside her window.

She sits bolt upright in bed. Out of the corner of her eye, she sees a man dashing away into the darkness.

A man who looks an awful lot like Andrew.

Tonja lets out a piercing scream.

Jon runs back into the bedroom. "What the—what happened? Are you okay?"

Tonja stutters, frantically pointing, forcing out the words. "He w-was...I saw...*Andrew!*"

Jon rushes to the window, looks out, left and right. But he sees nothing.

With a gentle sigh, he sits down on the bed next to Tonja and puts an arm around her quivering shoulders. "There's nobody out there. See? It was probably just a shadow."

Tonja shuts her eyes, desperately wanting to believe that's the truth.

Petrified that it's not.

CHAPTER 13

THE FIRST CALL COMES on a Tuesday.

Tonja is on her way out the door to her evening real estate class when the phone rings. Her landline was just installed a few weeks ago, and only Jon, Lisa, her parents, and a few close friends have the number.

Tonja answers with a chipper "Hello?"

But all she hears is silence—then a man slowly breathing.

"Hello?" she says again. "Is someone there? Andrew?"

Click. The line goes dead.

Tonja tries to put the call out of her mind. Maybe it was just a wrong number.

But two days later, it happens again.

The day after that, it happens twice.

Soon, Tonja is getting five, six, sometimes eight unsettling calls like this every day, at all hours, often in the middle of the night. Tonja and Jon are pretty damn concerned about it—but the Ventura County Sheriff's Office basically tells them to go jump in the ocean. Unless Andrew starts escalating things—making verbal threats against Tonja, harassing her, physically stalking her, or worse—there isn't much they can do.

"That's such bullshit!" Jon Balden exclaims after they hang up with the police. "The guy's nuts, but the cops are just going to sit back and do nothing? Maybe I should go talk to Andrew myself, tell him to cut out the crap or else."

"Jon, no," Tonja pleads. "Then he'll realize we're together. And you know that would only make things worse. I won't let you get dragged into this. Please."

But barely a week later, their secret is blown.

It's a Saturday night, and Jon and Tonja are sitting together on her couch, flipping through channels. They've decided that until things with Andrew cool off, it's best for them to lay low. That means not going out together and not spending any time at Jon's house, which is only a few feet from Andrew's.

Normally when they're in her apartment, they keep all the windows shut and all the blinds and curtains drawn tight. But it's the middle of August. A heat wave is pushing temperatures to ninety, and Tonja's place doesn't have air-conditioning. Reluctantly, she agreed to open some of her windows just a crack to let in the evening breeze.

She goes to the kitchen during a commercial to get

some water, and Jon hears her scream, "Oh my God! Oh my God!"

He leaps to his feet and races into the kitchen. To his horror, he sees Andrew standing right outside the open window, staring in.

Each man is completely shocked to see the other there.

"Jon?" Andrew exclaims.

"You son of a bitch!" Jon yells back. Instinctively, he grabs a knife from the block on the counter, then runs outside.

Is he going to hurt Andrew, Tonja wonders, *or just scare him off?*

Thankfully, he's long gone when Jon gets outside— no violence necessary. And they don't see Andrew at Tonja's apartment again.

But two weeks later, he does something even more heinous.

Jon is sitting in his office when he gets a frantic call from Tonja, who is sobbing. She can barely get the words out, but Jon pieces together that Andrew has left some kind of note under the windshield wiper of Tonja's car.

When Jon sees it later that day, he's horrified.

It's a long, rambling screed written in Andrew's childish chicken scratch. In it, Andrew professes his undying love for Tonja over and over. He doesn't apologize for anything he's done. Instead, he says he wants to flee the country with her so they can be together again—right after he murders Jon and burns down his house.

For Tonja and Jon, this literal death threat is the final straw. Tonja insists they go to the police again, and they do. They meet with a detective, give their statements, file a report.

But Jon isn't holding his breath. He has another idea.

He and Tonja have been dating for a while now, and they recently began talking about moving in together. Now seems like the perfect time to take that plunge. To make a fresh start.

Tonja had been hesitant to get so serious with another new partner so soon after Andrew. But she loves Jon deeply. She feels safe around him. And she wants desperately to rebuild her life, this time with him. So she runs the idea by her sister, and Lisa gives her little sister her enthusiastic blessing.

Just a few weeks later, Tonja, Jon, and Lisa are lugging cardboard boxes yet again—into Tonja and Jon's new hillside cottage. It's located in the city of Ventura, about fourteen miles from Mussel Shoals. But it feels like a world apart.

Tonja and Jon couldn't be happier with their decision to move and get away from Andrew Luster—before it was too late.

CHAPTER 14

July 14, 2000. Four Years Later

ANDREW LUSTER STANDS BUCK-NAKED in front of his open closet. He's thumbing through his vast collection of clothes, whispering, "What to wear, what to wear?"

Andrew likes to look his best when he goes out, but he isn't a particularly stylish or daring dresser. He mostly chooses his outfits based on how they make him feel—and the vivid memories each article stirs in him.

There's the checkered button-down he wore the evening he took home Stacey, a bubbly, redheaded Berkeley coed who was in town visiting friends at UCSB. The beige cardigan he was in when a casting session with Charlotte, a starving actress from Atlanta with peroxide-blond hair, ended up back at her apartment. The gray henley he had on when he met Nadine, a French au pair working for a wealthy family in Montecito, and made love to her in the back of his SUV. The navy polo he was wearing the night he met Tonja.

Tonja.

Andrew rubs the fine fabric between his fingers, recalling their magical first encounter and the passionate, turbulent months that followed.

He had actually kind of cared about that girl, at least before she'd turned all paranoid-controlling-psycho on him. Whining whenever he went out. Pestering him for every last detail of what he'd been doing. Messing with his stuff. And then, despite everything he'd given her, *she* had the gall to leave *him*—after cheating on him with his former friend. And then she'd totally shut him out of her life, wouldn't take his calls, even went to the goddamn *police* after he wrote her a heartfelt letter saying he forgave her and still loved her and would do anything to have her back.

"Stupid bitch," Andrew growls.

He pushes the blue polo aside and almost instantly his rage begins to fade. That was all a long time ago. Three years? Four? Water under the bridge. Whatever Tonja's doing now—and *whoever* she's doing now—Andrew hopes she's happy.

Yeah, right. He hopes she's miserable as shit.

Andrew continues sifting through his wardrobe until he finally finds the perfect shirt. It's white linen, soft and flowy, ideal for a hot July evening like this one. He bought it just a few weeks ago and hasn't worn it out yet.

Perfect, he thinks. *Let's go make some memories.*

About forty minutes later, Andrew has parked his green SUV and is strolling down State Street. He's scoping out the bar scene, making a mental plan of attack.

When Andrew passes O'Malley's, he hears peals of laughter coming from inside. He usually stays clear of this noisy, trashy Irish-pub wannabe, but for some reason, tonight he feels drawn to it. Seeing a long line of summer-semester UCSB girls waiting to get in doesn't hurt.

Andrew confidently strolls up to the bouncer at the front door. Before this beefy gentleman in a too-tight green T-shirt even has the chance to turn him away, Andrew slips a hundred-dollar bill into his massive paw. Works like a charm.

Once inside, Andrew posts up at the bar and scans the room like a lion hiding in the grass surveying a herd of gazelles, searching out the weakest one. He eyes the bevy of beautiful, tipsy college girls partying all around him.

He's been doing this long enough to know exactly what he's looking for.

And it doesn't take long to spot her.

Grooving with some girlfriends on the dance floor is a pretty girl with fair skin and long, honey-colored hair. She's wearing a black tube top that shows off her toned tummy, and a denim miniskirt that shows off almost everything else.

But it's her dancing that gives her away as an easy mark. It's confident but slightly awkward. Sexy but girlish. Andrew senses she's a young woman who isn't quite sure of herself yet and might respond well to the charms of an older man.

"Bartender?" he calls. He slides him a twenty. "One glass of ice water."

As Andrew waits for his beverage, he subtly reaches into the left pocket of his shorts.

He palms a glass vial filled with a clear liquid and carefully unscrews the cap.

CHAPTER 15

Three Days Later

CAREY EXPECTED THE OUTSIDE of the Ventura County Sheriff's Office to be grim. Intimidating. Instead, it's blandly pleasant, with red roof tiles and a manicured lawn. Its entrance is an automatic sliding glass door, the same as at the 7-Eleven attached to the campus student center.

Somehow, all this makes the situation Carey finds herself in even more surreal. And unbearable.

She stands there on the curb for a good five minutes watching the sliding doors open and close, open and close, digging her nails into her sweaty palms, trying desperately to slow her pounding heart and work up the nerve to go inside.

When she finally enters the lobby, the brusque, uniformed male desk sergeant grumbles, "Can I help you?"

"Uh...yes. I'm here to see, um, Detective Smith?"

"You asking me? She expecting you?"

Carey flinches at the deputy's rude tone and suddenly starts regretting this whole thing.

At first Carey had just wanted to put the entire awful episode out of her mind. Forget about it, move on. But her best friend convinced her to call the police this morning. She even offered to skip class this afternoon and go with her, but Carey said no. She needs to do this on her own. Needs to prove—to herself, to the world, to the pig that drugged and raped her—that she's strong. That she isn't afraid.

Carey takes a breath and answers slowly and firmly, "I have an appointment."

The sergeant grunts and picks up a phone. "Take a seat."

A few minutes later, Detective Melissa Smith appears from a side door. Middle-aged, African-American, dressed in a conservative charcoal blazer and wearing horn-rim glasses, Smith looks more like a stern librarian than a sex crimes investigator—until you see the gold badge and Glock nine-millimeter resting on her hip. "Carey? Hi, I'm Detective Smith. We spoke on the phone. Come on back."

Smith leads Carey down a quiet, sterile corridor lined with cubicles, many of them empty. It's a far cry from the bustling bullpen Carey expected after all the TV crime dramas she watches. They enter a private conference room and sit down at a long, polished glass table. Smith takes out a notepad and pen.

"Thanks again for reaching out, Carey. I know how difficult that must have been. You did the right thing. I'm going to ask you to tell me exactly what happened in as much detail as you can, okay?"

Fiddling with the drawstring of the UCSB hoodie she's wearing, Carey nods.

"Can I get you anything before we start? Coffee? Tea? A glass of water?"

Carey swallows hard. For a moment, she can't answer. "That...that's how it all started," she finally says. "That's the last thing I remember."

Smith leans in, her interest piqued. "Walk me through it."

"Like I told you on the phone, on Friday I was out with some friends, and this guy just comes up to me while I'm dancing. He was tall. Sort of cute, I guess. But he was old. I mean, not *old*-old. Like, in his thirties maybe? Anyway, he hands me a glass of water and starts asking all these questions about my life and telling me all about his. He was friendly. Kind of nice, actually. The next thing I know...I'm totally naked. In a shower. *His* shower. Like, at his house. But I didn't know where I was yet. My head was throbbing. I could barely stand up. Then he gets into the shower with me. He's naked too. I tried to tell him no. But I was so weak. So confused. So...so scared. And then he...he..." Carey squeezes her eyes shut. The rest is too painful to recount.

Smith nods and gives Carey a moment to compose herself. "What happened next?"

"Honestly, he acted like *nothing* had happened. I wanted to go home, but it was the middle of the night. I was still so tired. And I didn't know where I was. He gave me an old T-shirt to wear and I fell asleep on his couch. The next morning . . . he made me breakfast. Coffee, eggs, toast. I couldn't eat a bite. Then he gave me his number. He said he wanted to drive me back to my dorm but I told him no, so he called me a cab. Even gave me some cash to pay for it. That was the last time I talked to him."

Smith makes some notes in her pad, then flips back a few pages. "You said he told you his name was Andrew, correct? And he drove a dark green SUV?"

"Yes. I think so. I saw it in his driveway in the morning."

"I did some digging after we spoke," Smith says. "Ran the phone number you said he gave you. And I contacted a few local cab companies to verify where you were picked up. Everything checks out. I'm quite confident I've identified the suspect."

"That's good, right?"

Smith shuts her notepad and folds her hands on top.

"The man who assaulted you, Carey . . . there are some things you should know."

HIS NAME IS ANDREW LUSTER," Detective Melissa Smith continues. "Does that mean anything to you?" Carey shakes her head. "What about the name Max Factor?"

Carey thinks for a moment. "You mean, like, the makeup brand?"

"Luster is one of the great-grandsons of the company's founder. He and his family are extremely well connected. And very, very wealthy."

Carey nods but isn't sure where Detective Smith is going with this.

"As for the drug he used," Smith continues, "your symptoms—blacking out, grogginess, memory loss— it sounds like you were given gamma-hydroxybutyric acid."

"Gamma...what?"

"GHB. Liquid X. It's colorless, odorless, very easy to

slip into a drink. And it's completely flushed out of your system in about twelve hours, gone without a trace."

Carey's eyebrows furrow. "I don't understand what you're trying to say, Detective. So what if he's rich? So what if GHB doesn't stay in your body? You know his name. You know where he lives. He drugged me and raped me! Go arrest him! Unless...you don't believe me?"

Smith sighs. "I do believe you, Carey. But it's not me you'll have to convince. If this case goes to trial, Luster is going to hire a team of the best defense attorneys in the state. They're going to rip you apart on the stand. They're going to say Andrew *didn't* drug you. That you're making it up. That you went home with him willingly."

Carey absorbs Smith's words. Her lower lip begins to quiver. "But...but that's not true!"

"I know. Listen, I'm on your side. I want to see this man rot in prison. But these kinds of crimes can be impossible to prove in court. I want you to understand the reality of the situation and what we're up against here. Without evidence, it's your word against his."

Carey sags, shocked and overwhelmed. She had come to the police station to feel whole again, to reclaim her power, but now she feels even smaller. Helpless.

"What kind of proof would you need?" Carey asks.

Smith stares at Carey like she's sizing her up, weighing whether she's got it in her. "The question is, what would you be willing to do to get it?"

Without any hesitation, Carey exclaims, "Anything!"

Smith has her answer. "In that case, I have an idea. But it won't be easy."

That's a massive understatement. What the detective tells Carey she wants her to do makes the poor girl's stomach churn.

What Smith wants is for Carey to telephone the man who assaulted her, and have a friendly chat.

It's a common investigative technique, Smith explains, known as a "cool call." While the police listen in and record it, a victim phones a suspect, acts casual and cool like nothing happened, and gets him to admit— on tape—to having committed a crime.

In this instance, Carey needs to make Andrew confirm both that they had sex *and* that he drugged her—without making him suspicious that the line is bugged.

It's a very tall order. But Carey nervously agrees to give it a try.

Smith leads Carey into another, smaller conference room down the hall, this one filled with high-tech surveillance and audio-recording equipment. A second plainclothes detective, who introduces himself as Detective Dodd and tells her he's a digital forensics specialist, is seated at a laptop connected to a wireless telephone and multiple pairs of headphones.

Smith goes over some pointers and possible questions Carey might want to ask but says that where the conversation goes is up to her; she should just stay calm and act natural.

Finally Smith asks, "Okay, are you ready to do this thing?"

Carey swallows her fear and vigorously nods.

Smith hands Carey the phone, and she and Dodd put on headphones. Dodd types, then gives them the signal. Carey puts the receiver to her ear. It's ringing.

"Hello?" says a male voice on the other end.

The voice hits Carey like a punch to the gut. *It's him.* The person she hates more than anyone in the world. She's suddenly flooded with emotions—rage, doubt, fear.

Smith gives Carey a reassuring look.

"Uh...hi. Andrew? This is Carey. From Friday night? We met at O'Malley's?"

"Oh, hey! That was a fun night. How are you?"

"Uh...I'm...good. So, I wanted to ask you...what did you put in my drink?"

"Liquid X."

"Liquid X?"

"Yeah."

Carey looks over at Smith, who gives her a thumbs-up. So far, so good.

"Did you like it?" Andrew asks. "Makes you feel great, right?"

"Uh, yeah, totally," Carey answers. "I was wondering

if maybe...um...I could...I mean, *we* could, like, hang out and, uh, do it again?"

There's a long pause. *Shit.* Does Andrew suspect something?

"Why are you talking so weird?" he asks.

"I'm not!" Carey blurts out. "I just...really want to see you again. I had fun. And you don't have to drug me to have sex with me this time, okay?"

Andrew laughs like what he did was no big deal. Like it was all a big joke. "Okay. You got it. How about Saturday?"

Carey, tears in her eyes, looks over at Smith, who pumps her fist in victory.

They got the bastard. He's going down.

CHAPTER 17

July 18, 2000

ANDREW LUSTER SLIDES out of bed and reaches for the sky. He bends over and touches his toes. He squats, stands, extends his arms, and arches his back.

Outside his bedroom window, the bloodred morning sun is just starting to rise over the gently churning waves. The perfect time and conditions for a surf.

His body nice and limber, Andrew heads into the living room. He slips into his wetsuit, grabs his board, starts to head out—and stops dead in his tracks.

He hears the sound of approaching sirens.

Looking through his front windows, Andrew sees a fleet of police cruisers and SUVs screeching to a halt. Over a dozen uniformed deputies and plainclothes detectives get out and approach his front door.

One of them—a stern African-American woman in glasses—pounds on it. "Ventura County Sheriff's Office! Search warrant!"

Andrew doesn't panic. He doesn't even break a sweat. He makes an irritated noise. *They got the wrong house,* he thinks. *Idiots.*

He saunters over to the door and opens it.

"Andrew Stuart Luster?" says the woman. She holds up a badge and a typed document. "We're here to execute a search warrant on your home and premises. Please step outside."

"Hang on," Andrew says. "What's this all about? What gives you the right—"

"If you refuse, Mr. Luster, or attempt to interfere with our work in any way, you will be detained."

Now Andrew starts to stew. But what choice does he have?

Forced to wait in the back of a squad car parked in his driveway, he watches as the cops tear his home apart like a pack of vermin.

"What the hell are you guys even looking for?" Andrew asks the stone-faced deputy assigned to keep an eye on him. Infuriatingly, the cop just shrugs.

Meanwhile, inside, Detective Melissa Smith is overseeing the search, which is quickly turning into one of the most fruitful—and shocking—she's ever been part of.

The cops rifle through every drawer and cabinet. They flip through the pages of every book and magazine. They check under his couch cushions, then rip out the stuffing in them. They pull up the rug. Go through the trash. They even take apart and drain his toilet.

In the living room, latex-gloved detectives are photographing and testing a trove of pills, powders, and potions, including about twenty small vials containing a clear liquid.

So far, investigators have identified marijuana, cocaine, quaaludes, and psychedelic mushrooms. Smith stares intently as a detective places a GHB testing strip into one of the vials. It immediately turns from white to purple. Bingo.

In Andrew's bedroom, detectives make an unexpected discovery.

Smith watches her team photograph and place into plastic evidence bags two butterfly knives, a switchblade, a set of brass knuckles, and a pair of nunchakus. She's aware that Andrew makes movies, so there's a chance they might be props.

But they're not. They're all highly dangerous, illegal weapons.

"Hang on, got one more back here," says one of the investigators. "It's a doozy." He pushes aside a pile of clothes and shines his flashlight on an AK-47 assault rifle.

"*Please* tell me that's not real."

With his gloved hands, the detective carefully inspects the massive weapon. "Sorry, ma'am. Not loaded. But definitely not a fake."

Smith wanders back into the living room, feeling a little shaken. She knew Andrew Luster was a twisted sexual predator. But what else is he capable of?

"Detective Smith?" says a voice nearby. "You need to see this."

There's more? Smith thinks with dread as she steps into a small, cluttered storage closet being searched by her colleague Detective Galvez.

Her eyes widen when she sees it: a wall covered with photographs of beautiful young women, almost all wearing tight dresses, bikinis, or only their underwear. It's a chilling kaleidoscope of female flesh, especially in light of the accusations against Andrew. "Unbelievable," Smith says. "Could all these women be other victims?"

"Maybe," Galvez answers. "But that's not what I wanted to show you. I know our guy's a filmmaker but..." He gestures to a large plastic storage crate crammed with old VHS tapes. He picks up a few and shows Smith. "Each one is labeled with a different woman's name. Look—Helen, Stacey, Amy, Nadine, Megan, Katie, Tonja. We need to get these to the AV lab. Find out what's on them."

Smith looks down at the ground, fighting a sudden wave of nausea.

She has a terrible feeling she already knows what's on them.

CHAPTER 18

CAN I GET YOU anything before we start? Coffee? Tea? A glass of water?"

"How about you get me out of these goddamn cuffs!" Andrew Luster slams his shackled wrists down on the interrogation table. But Detective Melissa Smith doesn't flinch. In fact, she smirks. Which only makes Andrew angrier.

"You think this is funny?" he demands. "Barging into my house, harassing a private citizen, arresting me on a bunch of made-up charges?"

"Our search of your residence resulted in the seizure of numerous controlled substances and illegal weapons. Are you saying we made that up?"

"I'm saying that bitch is a liar! I didn't do any of the stuff she said."

"Walk me through *your* version of last Friday night's events, then. And I know you love being in front of the camera, but still, I'd like to remind you that this interview is being filmed, and you're entitled to remain silent or have a lawyer present."

"I don't need one. I've got nothing to hide. I'll tell you everything."

Smith leans back in her chair. Folds her arms. Gives him a look that says, *I'm all ears.*

"I was out at a bar. Struck up a conversation with a pretty girl. We went back to my place and had a great time. She even called me a couple days ago to hang out again. Now she's changing her story. It's bullshit. You see what's happening here, right?"

"No, Mr. Luster. Why don't you tell me."

"Extortion! A broke young college girl. A rich older guy. She's after my money. Wants me to pay her off. Simple as that." Andrew shakes his head in disgust.

So does Detective Smith—on the inside. "I'd like to talk now about the seventeen videotapes we found in your closet."

"Sure. Have you watched them?"

Smith's jaw tightens. "We've started to."

"Relax. Those movies are all just harmless fun."

"You're confident, Mr. Luster, that each of those women fully consented to being—"

"A hundred percent. They loved it!"

Smith can feel her blood pressure rising. Andrew's cavalier attitude about what she's seen on those tapes is, in a word, appalling. But Smith stays cool. Continues laying her trap. "So you never gave any of them, say, GHB?"

"Liquid X? We'd take it sometimes before a shoot. But only if they wanted to."

"Did you film a video with Carey on Friday?"

Andrew shakes his head. "We made love *off* camera. In the shower. Not that it's any of your damn business."

"Did you give her any liquid X that night? Slip anything in her drink?"

"No way."

"Did you *tell* her that you put liquid X in her drink?"

Andrew chuckles. What a weird question. "I never told her that, no."

It takes all of Smith's years of professional training to keep from leaping out of her seat in celebration. Andrew has no idea the police recorded Carey's cool call to him, the one in which he *did* tell her that. Now Smith has him on video lying about it. Any shred of credibility Andrew might have had just went up in flames. "That's all for now, Mr. Luster. Excuse me."

Smith exits the interrogation room and steps into the hallway.

Detective Galvez is waiting outside. "How'd it go?"

Smith answers with a dismissive nod. There are more important things to discuss. "Luster's address book, the one we recovered in the search—"

"The one filled with the first names and numbers of over a hundred women?"

Smith's expression turns grim. "Yes. We need to start going through it. Right away. We have to identify and contact every single woman in there. I want to get the word out to the local press too. Newspapers, TV, all of it. Luster isn't just a serial rapist. He's something a whole lot worse."

CHAPTER 19

A Week Later

BABE? ARE YOU HOME?"

Tonja, her arms laden with shopping bags, shuffles in through the front door.

Her husband appears at the top of the stairs. "Let me take those for you," Jon Balden says, hurrying down to help. "You shouldn't be carrying that much anyway. What did you get?"

"Some pork chops for dinner. Some cereal. Eggs. Toilet paper. And, okay, I might have picked up a few more little things for the nursery."

Jon laughs as he takes the bags from Tonja, revealing her bulging pregnant belly. "We have so much baby stuff, we're going to need to have a second kid!" He leans in and gives his wife a kiss, then brings the bags into the kitchen.

Tonja waddles into the living room. After a long day, all she wants to do is kick off her heels and plop down on the sofa. Being pregnant *and* working full-time as a real estate agent is exhausting.

As she makes a beeline for the sofa, she notices that the little red light on their answering machine is blinking. "Hon?" she calls to Jon. "Who's the new message from?"

"I don't know," he answers, joining her in the living room. "I didn't check it yet."

Tonja presses Play. It's from Lisa.

"Hey, guys, just seeing how you're doing. I'm sure you saw that awful thing in the paper today about...you know who. Crazy, right? Anyway, call me."

Tonja and Jon share a quizzical look. What's Lisa talking about?

Jon heads back into the kitchen and grabs the latest issue of the *Ventura County Star,* sitting unopened next to the day's mail. He flips through it until he sees the article—and gasps.

"Babe?" Tonja calls from the other room. "What is it?"

Jon heads back into the living room and shows her.

The headline reads "Cosmetics Heir Facing Rape, Poisoning, Drug and Weapons Charges."

Printed beside it is the mug shot of a scowling Andrew Luster.

Now it's Tonja's turn to gasp. In shock, she reads about Andrew's arrest and alleged crimes. She experiences the same toxic slurry of rage, betrayal, and fear she felt four years ago, back when he was still stalking and harassing her.

"Did you see this last part?" she asks Jon. "It says the police think there may be more victims. They're asking people who have information about Andrew or any connection to him to give them a call. Do you think I should?"

Jon pinches the bridge of his nose. "Honestly? I don't know. Do you really want to reopen this can of worms?"

"But if there are other women out there who he hurt that I can help in any way, I can't just sit back and do nothing."

Jon urges his wife to take some time to think. But Tonja's mind is already made up.

The next morning, before she goes to work, she pays a visit to the Ventura County Sheriff's Office. Once past the building's sliding glass doors, she informs the desk sergeant why she's there, then takes a seat in the lobby and waits. Not long after, a female detective comes out to greet her.

"Mrs. Balden? I'm Detective Smith. Thanks for..." As the detective shakes Tonja's hand, her words trail off and an odd expression crosses her face. "I—I'm sorry," Smith stutters. "Thank you for coming down."

"Is everything all right?" Tonja asks. "You look like you just saw a ghost."

Smith gives an evasive smile. "I pulled the complaint you and your husband filed about Mr. Luster four years ago. I'd like to ask you some additional questions about that. But first...would you be willing to watch a video-tape, Mrs. Balden, and...identify yourself in it?"

Tonja laughs uncertainly. "God, Andrew was *obsessed* with videotaping everything back then. He filmed me all the time when we were together. It drove me nuts," she says.

Detective Smith doesn't laugh along with her, and Tonja suddenly feels a pang of dread. She wishes she could turn to Jon for support right now, wishes he were by her side. "What kind of videos did you find?" she asks, her cheeks flushing at the sudden memory of a more risqué tape Andrew had once filmed of the two of them together.

"It's probably best if you see for yourself," Detective Smith says.

"I...I think I'd like to call my husband first. I want him to be with me when I—"

"Mrs. Balden?" Smith interrupts. "You don't ever want your husband to see this."

CHAPTER 20

INSIDE THE SMALL, WINDOWLESS conference room, Tonja Balden nervously lowers herself into a desk chair facing a television monitor. The screen is blank, but it's connected by a tangle of cords to a laptop. A plainclothes deputy named Detective Dodd is typing away at it. Another officer, Detective Galvez, is also present.

Detective Melissa Smith sits beside Tonja. She gives her a moment to get settled.

"Remember, we can stop the tape at any time. Are you ready?"

Tonja wipes a bead of cold sweat from her brow, then nods.

Smith and Dodd share a look. The TV screen flickers to life.

The footage is grainy at first, blurry and terribly shaky—until the camera is affixed to a tripod.

Immediately the image stabilizes and comes into focus.

It's a medium shot of a queen-size bed.

Despite the low lighting, a woman with curly strawberry-blond hair is clearly visible lying on top of the gray duvet cover.

Her head is turned away from the camera, her identity impossible to discern, but she's wearing a magenta-and-white floral-print dress, and, with a creeping feeling of dread, Tonja leans forward in her chair, scrutinizing the screen.

It takes her a moment, but then she recognizes that dress.

It's the one she borrowed from Lisa four years ago for her first night out in Santa Barbara.

"Is that...me?" Tonja asks Smith, protectively placing her hands on her pregnant belly.

"You tell us."

But Tonja doesn't have to. Her expression—stunned, nauseated, panicked—confirms to the detectives that it is.

The camera stays on Tonja alone for a few more interminable seconds.

Then Andrew Luster appears.

He calmly enters the frame and sits down on the edge of the mattress. He takes a long drag of what appears to be a rolled joint, then looks directly into the camera and flashes a chilling, serpentine grin.

"I dream about this," he says in a ghostly monotone. "A strawberry-blond, beautiful girl, passed out on my bed...basically there to do...*whatever I choose.*"

Andrew turns his attention to Tonja, lying behind him, as still as a corpse.

He reaches over and tickles the tops of her thighs. No response. Slowly, he traces his hands up her legs and teasingly but fully lifts up her skirt. He rolls her nylons down to her knees, then pulls down her underwear.

Through it all, on-screen Tonja doesn't move a muscle.

But the real Tonja lets out a horrified gasp. "Oh my God!" she exclaims. "What is he—no, no! Stop it!" she tells the man in the video.

Of course her pleas are futile. This footage was shot four years ago when Tonja was completely incapacitated by a powerful drug and Andrew was in total control.

It takes all of Tonja's strength not to look away as Andrew continues this abhorrent sexual assault on her unresponsive body.

When he's finally finished, Andrew painstakingly puts Tonja's underwear and nylons back in place, then gently smooths the fabric of her magenta dress. He gives her one last kiss, stands, and shuts off the camera. The screen blinks off.

Tonja sits there for a moment, almost as motionless as she appeared in the footage. She's struggling to process the avalanche of horror she's just seen.

She feels repulsed. Violated. Devastated. She has literally just witnessed her own rape—a rape that, until now, she never even knew had happened.

"How...how could he do that?" Tonja whimpers.

Smith places a consoling hand on her shoulder. "I can't even imagine how difficult that must have been to watch, Mrs. Balden. I just have one more question for right now. I know you and Mr. Luster dated and lived together for a number of months. We're trying to work out a timeline of his crimes, so do you have any idea when this tape might have been recorded?"

Only now does Tonja's numbness start to wear off. She breaks down in sobs. "It...it was the very first night we met! We went back to his place. He made us margaritas. With liquid X in them. Then he...he...did *this*. I had no idea! I never did. Jesus, I moved in with him three weeks later. I fell in love with him! How could Andrew have a normal *relationship* with me after..."

Tonja trails off, overcome by anguish and betrayal.

Smith shares a frigid look with Dodd and Galvez.

Andrew Luster might be even sicker than they realized.

CHAPTER 21

ALL RISE! CASE NUMBER CR-four-nine-two-five-nine, *The People versus Andrew Stuart Luster*. The Honorable Judge Ken W. Riley presiding."

People shuffle to their feet as Judge Riley enters this mahogany-lined courtroom and takes his vaunted perch behind the bench. With his round spectacles and rosy cheeks, he has the appearance of an avuncular high-school Latin teacher. But his bearing is sour, his control of his courtroom absolute, and his patience thin.

"Good morning. Unless there are any new motions, let's get started. Mr. Luster, how do you plead?"

Andrew Luster clears his throat, buttons the jacket of his dark Gucci suit, and picks a piece of lint off his blue-striped Armani tie. If he feels uncomfortable, he hides it with a smug, entitled smile. Standing beside Andrew is his high-priced lawyer Roger Diamond, a fiery Los Angeles criminal defense attorney with a reputation for being as vicious as a python and as unpredictable as his mop of unruly, uncombed gray hair.

"Your Honor," Andrew snarls, "I am angry and I am insulted, but I am *not* guilty."

"Bailiff," the judge says, "send the defendant some flowers, see if we can't cheer him up." Chuckles from the courtroom. "Moving on to the matter of bail. Counselor?" Judge Riley looks to the Ventura County senior deputy district attorney seated at the plaintiff's table: Maeve Fox, a prim, sharp veteran prosecutor.

"Maeve Fox for the People, Your Honor," she says, standing. "I would like to begin by reminding the court of the grievous, heinous nature of the array of crimes the defendant has been charged with. Among them, the drugging and aggravated sexual assault of three innocent young women whom he secretly filmed without their consent for future perverted viewing."

Sitting in the back of the gallery, Detective Melissa Smith shakes her head.

The police had found *seventeen* videotapes showing Andrew engaging in sex acts with different unconscious women. That's in addition to all the *other* women whose pictures hung on the wall of his closet and the over one hundred women listed by their first names in his little black book. And God knows how many more.

Smith is confident that Andrew drugged and assaulted many, many other women. She had hoped charges would be filed against him on behalf of *all* the others. But the system just doesn't work like that.

Detectives Smith and Galvez and their team had worked for weeks to chase down and identify every victim. It proved to be a nearly impossible task. In the end, they were able to build only one more case, in addition to Carey's and Tonja's, against Andrew: his rape of a local high-school student, who was only seventeen when she met Andrew on the beach and went back to his bungalow to have some drinks.

Because the victim was underage at the time, Judge Riley allowed her to be referred to in court filings as Shawna Doe. Carey and Tonja, too, petitioned and were granted the right to remain anonymous.

Still, Luster has been charged with eighty-six separate criminal counts, including rape, sexual battery, sodomy, and poisoning. If he's found guilty on even a handful, he'll be facing over a century behind bars. That's some small comfort to Smith, but not much.

"It is indisputable," Fox continues, "that the defendant was and remains a highly dangerous threat, not only to this community, but to every single woman in the world. Furthermore, the People would note that the defendant is extremely personally wealthy. Facing the prospect of spending the rest of his natural life in prison, and with a multimillion-dollar trust fund at his fingertips, the People believe the defendant is an exceptionally high flight risk. We ask that bail be set at ten million dollars."

Only now does Andrew's cocky smile start to waver. Only now does it appear to hit him that he just might spend the rest of his days in jail.

"Thank you, Counselor. Mr. Diamond?"

As if sensing his client's fear, Andrew's lawyer leans over to him and whispers, "Relax. I'll have you home in time for dinner." Then he stands and addresses the judge. "Just ten million, Your Honor?" Diamond sneers. "Why not twenty? Fifty? A hundred?"

Andrew looks like he's wondering just what the hell his lawyer is doing.

"At that level, does it matter?" Diamond says. "My client may be affluent, but he can't afford anything close to that. And Ms. Fox knows it! She wants to lock up an innocent man and throw away the key. A man falsely accused by three vindictive gold diggers whose only crimes were being born into a wealthy family and enjoying the company of women. It's an outrage!"

"Save the theatrics for trial, Counselor," Judge Riley cautions. "What's your counteroffer to the government's bail request?"

"Actually, Your Honor, I had an idea..."

CHAPTER 22

ANDREW LUSTER SHUTS HIS eyes and takes a long, luxurious gulp of his drink. He moans in delight as the bubbles prick his tongue and slide down his throat. Never in his life has champagne tasted so good.

It tastes, in a word, like freedom.

"Roger, you're a goddamn genius! Cheers!" He clinks his glass against the can of ginger ale his attorney, who is sitting on the sofa beside him with a stack of documents on his knees, is holding.

Andrew downs the rest of his drink in one gulp, then pours himself another.

"Go easy on the sauce, would you?" Roger Diamond says. "We're not celebrating. We have a lot of work to do on your defense."

"Not celebrating? Shit, I could have been locked in there for months! Now I get to hang out here at home, and all I have to do is wear this little thing." Andrew hikes up the leg of his jeans to get another look at the bulky black electronic bracelet strapped around his left ankle.

In Ventura County, this kind of pretrial arrangement—house arrest with GPS monitoring—had previously been granted only to juveniles, kids who had committed minor infractions and who had school to attend and families to keep an eye on them. Incredibly, the silver-tongued Diamond was able to convince Judge Riley to allow its use for Luster. He also managed to lower Andrew's bail to a much more affordable one million dollars. As far as either of them can tell, Andrew is the first adult defendant in county history to be granted such a privilege. The deputy DA had been furious, grumbling that it was granted *because* of Andrew's privilege—his wealth, his status, his fancy, smooth-talking lawyer.

Diamond had just shrugged and taken it as a compliment.

"Hey, do you think this is waterproof?" Andrew asks. "I can still go surfing with this thing on, right? Might be tough to get my wetsuit on over it but—"

"Andrew. *Focus.*"

Diamond's harsh tone gets his client's attention.

"Listen to me. You're facing some very serious charges here. And because of who you are, who your *family* is, this case is already starting to get some national press. The DA's office is going to come at us hard. I'm very good at what I do, Andrew, but I can't do it alone. Understand?"

Over the next few hours, Andrew and Diamond put their heads together and formulate a defense strategy. They agree to portray Andrew as the real victim in all of this; they will claim that his accusers are simply three vengeful party girls who are only after his money.

Andrew grins. He's mesmerized by his lawyer's legal mind. The significant fees he's paying suddenly feel like a steal. "You're going to get me off, aren't you?" Andrew exclaims.

"Guilty people get off," Diamond replies. "Your case is still an uphill battle. But it's looking a whole lot better."

CHAPTER 23

December 2002

ROGER DIAMOND RISES AND approaches the witness stand, weary but determined.

He'd known the Luster case would be a doozy when he'd signed on over a year and a half ago. But he'd had no idea it would stretch on so long or take so much out of him.

After months of wrangling and countless motions and petitions, the trial finally got under way a few weeks ago. And so far, so good. Deputy District Attorney Maeve Fox has proven to be a shrewder prosecutor than he'd anticipated, but two of her three star witnesses—first Tonja, then Shawna—have withered under Diamond's surgically precise and devastating cross-examination.

Now it's his turn to question Carey. If Diamond can poke enough holes in her story to make even one member of the jury doubt her credibility, Andrew Luster just might walk.

"Good morning, Ms. Doe," Diamond says. "We all

know that's not your *real* last name. But what else are
you lying to us about?"

"Objection, argumentative," Fox snaps.

"Sustained," replies Judge Riley.

"Ms. Doe . . . like many young people your age, do you
have any student loans, outstanding credit card debt,
anything like that that you're working to pay off?"

"Um, some. I don't see what that has to do with—"

"And are you aware that my client has a net worth
well into the tens of millions?"

"I didn't know that when I met him."

"I asked if you're aware of it *presently.*"

"Yes."

"All right. Now take me back to the night you met
my client. What were your first impressions of him?"

"Um, I don't know. He was . . . weird. I was like, *Why
is this old guy trying to flirt with college girls?* He seemed
pretty creepy."

"That's interesting. Because that's not exactly what
you told the police, is it?" Diamond picks up a document on the defendant's table. "According to Detective
Smith's official report, you told her you had a long and
pleasant conversation with my client that night. You
accepted a beverage from him."

"It was just a glass of—"

"You liked him so much, in fact, that you decided to
go home with him. You described my client as 'cute,'
'friendly,' 'nice.' These are your words, aren't they?"

"Yes—I mean, no. He was fine, I guess. At the bar. But I didn't *decide* to go home with him. I didn't decide to do *anything* after he put—"

"Moving along, Ms. Doe. Your sexual encounter with my client happened on a Friday. Yet you didn't contact the sheriff's department until Monday. What took you so long to talk yourself into believing you had been violated?"

"Objection, badgering," Fox says.

"I'll rephrase. Why did you wait all that time to go to the police?"

"I . . . I don't know. I was in shock. In denial, maybe. I was scared."

"Scared? Scared of what? Scared of what your friends and family would say if they found out you had just taped a porn audition?"

"Objection!"

"Mr. Diamond, that's enough," barks Judge Riley.

Diamond has no further questions. Carey is dismissed from the stand, and she scurries out of the court-room, pointedly avoiding eye contact with Andrew, who has been watching his lawyer's questioning with muted glee.

"Awesome job," he whispers to Diamond as he sits down beside him.

"Don't look so happy," Diamond warns. "And we're not out of the woods yet."

Judge Riley adjourns for lunch. When court is back

in session, Fox rises to declare that the People's case is nearly complete. She has just one more exhibit to enter into evidence.

The tapes.

When she plays them, they go off in the courtroom like a truck bomb.

Diamond is powerless to object or redirect as Fox shows nearly ten excruciating minutes of vile, stomach-churning footage to the jury.

Tonja, Carey, and Shawna are each seen lying in Andrew's bed, unconscious, helpless, while he undresses them. Fondles them. Penetrates them. Sodomizes them. All while boasting out loud about how powerful it makes him feel. About the thrill of what he's doing and the sexual satisfaction it gives him. Either all three women are Oscar-caliber actresses or they've been drugged into a comatose state by one deeply depraved man.

Scanning all twelve shocked, revolted, traumatized faces of the jury, many of them in tears, Diamond fears his client's fate may be sealed.

CHAPTER 24

JUDGE RILEY DOESN'T SEEM like the type to get swept up in the holiday spirit, which is why it surprised defense attorney Roger Diamond when, one morning last week, he noticed the judge had placed a small, silver-tinsel Christmas tree at the edge of his bench.

Diamond is staring at it now, watching the fluorescent courtroom lighting bounce off its tiny fake branches as he listens to prosecutor Maeve Fox say, "Your Honor, the People rest."

Diamond starts to stand. He expects Judge Riley to ask him to begin presenting the defendant's side of the case.

Instead, the judge dismisses the jury for the remainder of the day, although he keeps the attorneys behind to discuss various administrative matters. Chief among them is the issue of whether to continue or alter Andrew Luster's bail agreement over the lengthy upcoming winter holiday.

"Your Honor," says Fox, "given that the court will be in recess for two weeks, the People ask that the defendant's house-arrest arrangement be suspended during that time and that he be remanded into the custody of a county correctional facility."

"Your Honor, I see no reason for this request," Diamond argues. "For the last eighteen months, my client has appeared at every hearing. He's done everything the court has asked of him. He's never violated a single term of his bail agreement. Not once."

"That's irrelevant," Fox counters. "The defendant was granted house arrest to allow him to be closer to this courthouse, Mr. Diamond, so you two could more easily work on his defense. With the court in recess, there's no need. Hence, jail."

"No need? The defense hasn't presented our case yet. We have a great deal to work on. In fact, I'd like to ask the court to *broaden* my client's travel privileges during the holiday to include my Los Angeles offices."

"Now that is just ridiculous," Fox fires back. "The defendant should be in jail."

"Your Honor, District Attorney Scrooge clearly just wants to lock my client up now while she still can because she knows she's going to lose on verdict."

"Oh, Roger, give me a break. Your client is about to get hit with a hundred and twenty years. You know it and he knows it. Is this court really supposed to trust him not to use his millions to flee the country during a two-week-long vacation?"

"Counselor," Judge Riley interjects, "I respect your concerns. But Mr. Diamond is right. The defendant has thus far complied with all his bail requirements impeccably. He's had eighteen months to, as you say, withdraw his millions and flee, but he hasn't. I see no reason to suspect he might do so now."

The normally cool and collected Fox begins to lose her temper. "Your Honor, I'm sorry, but you're wrong. Andrew Luster is going to jump bail. Mark my words. It's not a matter of *if* he's going to run, it's a matter of *when*. And we're telling you that now is the time."

But the judge isn't having it. "The People's motion to revoke the defendant's house arrest is denied. Further, the defense's motion to grant the defendant limited weekday travel and visitation rights to counsel's Los Angeles office is granted, with the imposition of an eight p.m. nightly curfew."

Fox's jaw drops. "Your Honor, you can't seriously be—"

"Now, if there's nothing else on the table, I have presents to wrap. We're adjourned."

Judge Riley bangs his gavel. Fox shoots Diamond a vicious look. Diamond responds with a victorious one, then returns to the defense table to gather up his files. He's expecting Andrew to be his usual boyish, upbeat self. Instead, he looks ashen. "Why the long face? Rather spend Christmas in the clink?"

"Did Fox really mean what she said up there?"

"Mean what?"

"That I'm gonna get a hundred and twenty years. That we both know it. You'd tell me if I was screwed, right, Roger?"

Diamond sighs. He hates having these conversations with clients. "Here's what I can tell you: I don't know. I've already instructed my office to begin preparing to file your appeal. We're going to be ready either way."

"An appeal? That doesn't fill me with a whole lotta confidence!"

Diamond takes Andrew by the shoulders. Looks into his eyes. "This thing isn't over yet. Anything can happen. *Anything.*"

Andrew listens to Diamond's words, but he doesn't seem comforted. Apparently, the stark reality of his situation is finally beginning to sink in.

"Now, go home," Diamond instructs. "Get some rest. We have only a few more court days before the holiday recess. I need you focused. Hear me?"

Andrew nods in agreement.

(Diamond realizes only later that his client's mind was elsewhere. *Plotting.*)

CHAPTER 25

January 3, 2003

ONE OF ANDREW LUSTER'S worst fears has been confirmed.

It was nearly impossible to put a skintight wetsuit on over a GPS-monitoring ankle bracelet.

So he'd improvised by cutting a long slit down the left calf of one of his older suits. It's a struggle to get into it, but at least he's still able to go surfing. Thank God the monitor is waterproof.

Today, out in the early-morning shallows, Andrew savors every precious moment of his favorite hobby even more than usual. The smell of the briny air. The rush of catching a wave. The peace and tranquility that only this act provides.

Traipsing back across the sand, his mind clear, Andrew makes a critical decision. He'd been waffling, but no longer. Today is the day.

Which means he has no time to waste.

Inside, after a quick shower, Andrew tosses two large suitcases onto his bed and starts stuffing them with clothes. Summer clothes. Where he's going, the temperature rarely dips below sixty-five. Next, he ransacks his house for valuables.

Andrew was never much for high-end antiques, but he does own a few ancient American Indian trinkets that he bought at an auction a few years ago for about eight thousand dollars. They've been collecting dust on his mantel ever since. He sweeps them into his arms and drops them on top of his clothing.

Andrew also has about six thousand dollars in cash stashed in a hollowed-out hardcover on his bookshelf. He rolls the bills up, puts a rubber band around them, and shoves the wad into his pocket.

Finally, he takes a long, painful look around his beloved little home. His bachelor pad. His love nest. His sanctuary. His prison cell. Decades of memories. Hundreds of women. Andrew silently says goodbye to all of it.

This may very well be the last time he sees it.

Andrew drags his suitcases outside and slides them into the back seat of his green SUV. He grabs the rusty old pair of garden shears he's been keeping on the floor mat of his vehicle for this very moment.

He places his left ankle on the bumper. Rolls up his jeans. Carefully slips the bracelet's band between the two blades. Then clamps them down hard.

The blades cut through the vulcanized rubber like butter. The black bracelet flops onto the gravel driveway and lies there like a dead bird.

And just like that, Andrew Luster is a free man again.

He hops behind the wheel, guns the engine, and pulls out of the driveway. After a few quick turns through his quiet neighborhood, he's cruising south on the 101 Freeway. It's a Friday—the last weekday of the holiday recess before his trial resumes on Monday—but it's early enough that traffic is moving smoothly.

Andrew opens all the windows, lets the highway wind roar around him.

He flips on the radio, finds a classic-rock anthem, and blares it.

Andrew is in a hurry, of course, but he's careful not to speed or change lanes without signaling. He doesn't want to do *anything* that might get him pulled over. In the past, he could often joke or charm his way out of a ticket. But now, he's a fugitive. He's not likely to have much luck now.

For the first thirteen miles or so, the 101 hugs the coastline, lush foothills on one side, crashing waves on the other. After passing the city of Ventura, the freeway heads inland, through endless scrubby sprawl. Andrew eventually veers south through Topanga Canyon, then merges onto the Pacific Coast Highway. As the name implies, it's a truly stunning drive, passing the tail end of Malibu and the heart of Pacific Palisades, two of the wealthiest communities in the country, with multimillion-dollar mansions perched precariously on the edges of the cliffs.

But Andrew doesn't have much time to enjoy the view.

If he keeps going in this direction, he'll soon reach another freeway, one that would take him across the city and deposit him in downtown LA, not far from Roger's office. He's made that trip a number of times since his bail terms were loosened.

But today, Andrew takes the exit for San Vicente Boulevard.

He coasts for a few blocks through the quiet residential streets of Santa Monica, a little coastal city that's part of greater Los Angeles. Spotting a pay phone on the corner of San Vicente and Tenth Street, he pulls over and parks under a broad, shady palm tree. Some two hours after leaving Mussel Shoals, Andrew gets out of his car. He grabs his bags. Approaches the phone. Picks up the receiver.

"Directory assistance," says the cheerful operator. "What city, please?"

"Los Angeles," Andrew replies. "I need a cab. *Now.*"

CHAPTER 26

YOU DON'T KNOW WHERE he is? Is this some kind of sick joke, Counselor?"

Roger Diamond is in the midst of an epic dressing-down from Judge Ken Riley, whose normally ruddy cheeks have turned the color of stoplights.

"I wish it were, Your Honor. But I don't have a clue. The last time I spoke to my client was Thursday. He didn't return my calls on Friday, but I didn't think anything of it. When he failed to check in with authorities for his eight o'clock curfew that evening, they went to his home and discovered that he and his vehicle were missing. I was flabbergasted."

Deputy DA Maeve Fox sniffs. "You fought for his bail. You spoke to him last. I don't have to tell you how this looks, Mr. Diamond."

"Counselor, I was doing my job. And I deeply resent that implication."

"You loosened Luster's leash and unlocked his cage," she responds. "You all but told him to run away!"

"Ms. Fox, I would remind you that my client is a human being. And I am as shocked and appalled by his absence as—"

"Enough!" Judge Riley booms. "Save this bickering for the schoolyard. I'll let the U.S. Marshals Service track down the defendant and investigate his manner of escape. Right now, I believe all of us in this courtroom want the same thing. A fair trial."

"Of course, Your Honor," Diamond agrees. "But under the circumstances, that's clearly impossible. You need to declare a mistrial."

"No, no, no. Your Honor, please," Fox pleads. "Think of all the testimony we've heard. How could I possibly put those poor women on the stand again? How could I ask them to relive the most painful experiences of their life? They deserve justice."

"I agree," Diamond says. "And my heart breaks for them. However—"

"Yeah, Roger, I'm sure it keeps you up at night. Your Honor, the defendant is the one who skipped bail. A mistrial would be rewarding him for it—and punishing his victims."

"It's not a reward," Diamond insists. "It's our only option. How can any defendant get a fair trial if it's conducted in his absence?"

Riley pushes his round glasses farther up the bridge

of his nose. "Counselor, I believe you've just answered your own question."

For once, the great Roger Diamond is left speechless.

"I . . . don't quite follow, Your Honor."

"The trial of Andrew Luster will continue . . . in absentia. Mr. Diamond, you will present your client's defense as scheduled as if he were right there beside you."

"I . . . I'm sorry, Your Honor, but that's absurd. The Hague tries war criminals in absentia. This is a superior court trying a sex offender!"

"Are you saying I don't have the authority to order it?"

"I'm saying that here in Ventura County, California, it just isn't done!"

Fox chimes in. "Putting an adult defendant on juvenile-style house arrest just isn't done in this county either, Counselor. That didn't seem to bother you before."

Diamond fumes. "Then, Your Honor, I refuse. If you insist on continuing this trial as a farce, I'll resign as defendant's counsel."

"You will do no such thing, Mr. Diamond. Unless you'd like to be held in contempt. Try me, Counselor. I dare you."

One of Diamond's most underrated skills as a defense attorney is knowing when to cut his losses and move on. Knowing when it's time to shut up.

This is one of those times.

"Bailiff? Please summon the jury back into the

courtroom. Mr. Diamond, prepare to call your first witness."

Gritting his teeth, Diamond returns to the defense table and collects his notes.

He glances over at the chair beside him—which is conspicuously, ominously empty.

CHAPTER 27

February 2003

DEPUTY DA MAEVE FOX turns to the jury and takes a slow, dramatic breath.

"First, you heard it in their own words. Three innocent young women. Three strangers. All with three remarkably similar stories. And all with the terrible misfortune of crossing paths with a monster. Maybe you had some doubts about their accounts. Maybe you noticed a few minor inconsistencies, even though you heard from two expert witnesses that after a person's been drugged, gaps in memory are common."

Fox paces to the other side of the jury box.

"But then, ladies and gentlemen, you saw the tapes. You saw things that no human being should ever see. Tapes the defendant made for his own sick pleasure while committing his despicable crimes. A picture, they say, is worth a thousand words. In this case? I say a video is worth a hundred and twenty-four years."

Fox gestures to the defense table, where Diamond sits alone.

"And what has the defendant had to say for himself? That's right. Nothing. Two weeks ago, he ran away from his beachside home. Why did he do it? Out of respect for the judicial process? Because he's prepared to accept responsibility and face the consequences of his actions? Of course not. The defendant ran because he's a coward. He's a fabulously wealthy man, accustomed to doing whatever he wants without consequence. Andrew Luster ran because he's *guilty.*"

Fox pauses, letting her words sink in for the twelve members of the jury.

"Ladies and gentlemen, you have the power that Mr. Luster's victims did not. You can make him pay. Guilty verdicts on all eighty-six counts would put him in prison for the rest of his life and keep him from hurting any other woman ever again."

Fox takes her seat at the prosecution's table. Judge Ken Riley calls on the defense to make its own closing statement.

For Roger Diamond, writing and rewriting this argument over the past few days has been a Herculean task. So has defending his absentee client over the past two weeks.

Diamond has tried his best to do this thankless job. He introduced into evidence some of Andrew's earlier professional soft-core feature films to establish his bona fides as a director. He also tried, unsuccessfully, to get permission to play another tape of Tonja, one in which she willingly took her top off while Andrew filmed.

Diamond picked apart photographs taken during the police search, suggesting that biased investigators, jealous of Andrew's wealth, might have planted evidence.

He called multiple expert witnesses to offer alternative theories of the women's claims of blackouts and memory loss.

In a last-ditch effort, he even put Andrew's own mother on the stand as a character witness.

But nothing can erase the simple, undeniable fact that his client has skipped bail—and has now been placed on the FBI's Most Wanted list.

This isn't just a single elephant in the courtroom. It's an elephant stampede.

"Guilty," Diamond says, buttoning his jacket and approaching the jury box, "until proven innocent. That's the core principle of our system of justice. But here, things are more complicated. The DA is right, ladies and gentlemen. My client *is* guilty . . . of violating the terms of his bail agreement. We can all see that with our own eyes. And if that's what he were on trial for today, the best defense attorney with the best closing statement in the world couldn't convince you otherwise."

Diamond brushes an errant lock of hair from his brow.

"But that's *not* what my client is on trial for today. And it is very, *very* important that all of you keep that in mind. When Andrew Luster is located, he *will* be punished for running bail. As he should be. But breaking one law *does not mean* you're guilty of breaking another. Only evidence proves that. And what evidence have we seen? A few made-up stories from some embarrassed, desperate women. A few so-called medical experts who never examined any of the women personally. A few minutes of homemade porn starring one actress who *admitted* to ingesting GHB with my client!"

Diamond glares at the jury now. "We're talking about a man's *life* here, ladies and gentlemen." He raises his voice for the big finish. "His life! Ask yourself: are you truly willing to sentence my client to die behind bars? Has the prosecution fully convinced you of these charges beyond a reasonable doubt? If you're even the slightest bit unsure, there's only one option. *Not guilty.* Thank you."

Diamond sighs and returns to his seat. He shoots a quick look at Fox, who offers him a nod of professional respect. Diamond returns it. Whatever the verdict, these two fierce legal warriors have fought valiantly to the bitter end.

Judge Riley gives the jury a few instructions, then releases them to deliberate.

Less than an hour later, they've reached unanimous verdicts on all eighty-six separate drug and sexual assault counts.

Guilty.

Guilty.

Guilty.

Judge Riley thanks the jury for their service. He notes that because he plans to order the sentences to be served consecutively, Andrew Luster will be facing over a hundred and twenty years in prison.

But if he isn't found and brought to justice, the fugitive Luster won't serve a single day.

CHAPTER 28

April 2003

TOWELING HIS THINNING WET hair, fresh from a late-morning swim, Min Labanauskas steps onto his second-floor balcony and gazes happily at his growing kingdom below.

Eight luxury casitas in various stages of construction, each with its own private patio and pool, are spread out before him along this rocky, picturesque coastline. Needing only paint jobs and landscaping, a few, like his own, are basically move-in ready. Others are little more than clusters of two-by-fours protruding from concrete foundations.

Just a few years ago, it might have been difficult for some to imagine that this barren strip of beach in the middle of nowhere—outside Punta de Mita, a tiny Mexican fishing village an hour north of Puerta Vallarta—would one day be transformed into Costa Custodio, a high-end private resort community.

But not for Min, a man of great vision, patience, and determination.

In a former life, he worked as a biophysicist at a major pharmaceutical company in Tucson, spending months, sometimes years, manipulating a single microscopic organism. Now retired, he and his wife, Mona, have thrown themselves—and their savings—into real estate development. And they've never looked back.

"Hola, Señor La Bamba, ¿qué tal?" calls Alejandro, the friendly property manager and construction foreman, as he pushes a wheelbarrow on the road below Min's balcony. He and many of the local workers Min hired had struggled to master his tongue-twisting Lithuanian surname, so they'd shortened it to La Bamba, which Min still gets a kick out of.

"Morning, Alejandro! The new mosaic work on number *cinco*—great job."

"Ah, yes, *gracias!*"

After shaving and dressing, Min grabs a stack of paperwork and a chilly cerveza and settles into a recliner in a shady spot beside his pool. Mona prefers to work in the air-conditioned front leasing office, but Min, after decades spent slaving away in gloomy, windowless laboratories, will never get tired of sunshine and fresh air.

Just before lunchtime, he hears his wife approaching. She's in the middle of a conversation with an American whose voice Min doesn't recognize.

"Honey?" she calls as she steps onto the patio. "I'd like you to meet someone."

Mona is standing with a tall, tan, strapping young man—at least, young to Min's sixty-five-year-old eyes—who's wearing sun-bleached shorts and a fraying tank top.

"Hi, David Carrera," the man says, giving Min a firm, two-handed shake. "A pleasure."

"He's a real estate developer from Hawaii," Mona explains.

"Born and raised. I wouldn't call myself a developer, though. I'm retired, like you guys. And looking to put some money into Mexican properties."

"Retired at your age?" Min asks, both impressed and a tiny bit envious. "Let me guess. You were one of those techie dot-com guys or something."

David laughs. "Not even close. Professional surfer."

David and Mona pull up recliners next to Min's, and for the next hour, the three talk business over a round of beers. It's quickly clear to Min that David is relatively new to the international real estate–investment game. But the way he tosses around terms like *amortization, alternative minimum tax,* and *housing-loan trust* tells him that his new friend might have more access to some real cash reserves than his beach-bum persona would suggest.

"Well, this has just been awesome, guys," David says. "So informative. I think I could really see myself investing in a community like this. And spending some time here."

"How about you start tonight?" Mona asks brightly.

"Great idea!" says Min. "We've got plenty of space. Our friends the Gordons are in casita *dos,* and the Feinsteins are in *tres.* But *cuatro's* empty. Some light fixtures aren't installed yet, and the stove isn't hooked up, but the master bedroom suite is all set. Stay, David. Have dinner with us. Spend the night. Get a feel for the place."

David considers the generous offer. "I'd love that. Thank you. But maybe we could share a meal tomorrow? I was thinking of checking out the bars in Puerto Vallarta tonight."

Mona clicks her tongue in disapproval. "Oh, David, you'd just hate it down there. It's a zoo. Nothing but college girls on spring break getting drunk and going wild."

David's lips form a thin, almost imperceptible smile. "You're right. Sounds terrible."

CHAPTER 29

May 2003

MIN HAS JUST CRACKED open a beer by the pool when he hears the phone ringing inside his casita. Grumbling, he goes in and answers it.

"Hello, Min? It's Lou. Are you sitting down?"

Lou Feinstein is one of Min's closest friends. He and his wife stayed with Min and Mona at Costa Custodio recently, but now they're back home in Florida.

"Of course I'm not sitting down. I just walked over to get the phone."

"Well, take a seat somewhere. I'll wait. You're not going to believe this."

"Just tell me, Lou. What is it?"

"Are you familiar with the program *America's Most Wanted*? Gloria and I were watching it last night and we recognized one of the people—David!"

"David? David who?"

"*David.* You know, that nice young fellow we had

dinner with. They say he's some kind of crazy sex pervert from California."

David Carrera? Now Min remembers him; the image is as clear as the water in his pool. He was the friendly, flaky, would-be real estate investor who'd spent a few nights at one of their casitas, though he hasn't come around since.

"You need to get your eyes checked, Lou. David's a surfer from Hawaii."

"Min, I'm telling you. His family's loaded and he's wanted by the FBI. Look it up!"

Min loves his friend, but the old man is starting to lose his marbles. He ends the call with a chuckle and tries to put it out of his mind.

But later that day, his curiosity gets the better of him.

Mostly to prove Lou wrong, Min navigates to the FBI's Most Wanted page—and nearly falls out of his chair when he sees David's mug shot staring back at him.

The man's real name is Andrew Luster. Min does some further research online and learns that Andrew was convicted of over eighty drug and rape charges, and he's been missing for four months. Min also stumbles across a video of a burly, fiftyish man with long blond hair who claims to be a bounty hunter and has vowed to track Luster down and bring him to justice no matter where in the world he is.

That's when Min remembers something else.

The last time they saw each other, he and David had exchanged contact information. Neither man ever reached out to the other, and Min assumes that slip of paper is long gone, but after a bit of rummaging, he finds it buried under a stack of files on his desk. David had scribbled down the phone number of what he said was an office he'd rented in the nearby city of Tepic.

Min breathlessly tells his wife everything, and the two debate what to do.

Mona wisely suggests calling the FBI's field office in Mexico City. After numerous fruitless attempts, they finally get a special agent on the line, but he seems skeptical of their story and sounds annoyed when he says, "We'll look into it."

Next they try the U.S. consulate in Guadalajara but manage only to leave a voice-mail message—which gets cut off in the middle.

A call to the local Mexican police headquarters is even less successful.

Min has half a mind to give up. He tells Mona that they have already wasted too much time trying to share their information with law enforcement agencies.

"*Wasted?*" Mona exclaims. "Honey, you read what that man did. He's a maniac! Those poor women. How awful. And don't forget, he lied to us too. We're a part of this now whether we like it or not. We need to help catch him!"

Min sighs. He knows his wife is right. But what more can they do?

Then he gets a crazy idea. He reopens his web browser.

"Dear? I want you to watch this video I found . . ."

CHAPTER 30

June 2003

¿*BUENO?*"

"David? Is that you? This is Min Labanauskas. How are ya?" Min holds his breath as he waits for the man on the other end of the phone to respond.

"Oh, hey there, Min. I'm good. You?"

"Well, to tell you the truth, I've been better. That's why I'm calling. It's one of my major investors. You're in the real estate business, so you know how it is. He'd been in for a bunch of units, but then his shipping business went under. So he's pulling out—and leaving me up shit's creek. It's a whole mess."

"That sucks, Min. You just never know who you can trust these days."

"Tell me about it," Min says. "Anyway, I remembered you'd been keen on owning a piece of Costa Custodio. Well, today's your lucky day. I can give you pretty

much as many units as you want for seventy cents on
the dollar. You'd be doing me a real favor."

"Really? That cheap? Does sound like a pretty good
deal."

"Listen, why don't you come by later? We can catch
up, have a few beers, and I'll run some numbers
for you."

"Actually, that would be great. I was thinking of
going surfing in Punta de Mita later anyway. I'll stop by
afterward."

"David, you're a gem! See you when I see you."

Min hangs up the phone and flashes a thumbs-up to
the man next to him.

"You did good, Mr. L. Real good." The scratchy bari-
tone belongs to Duane Lee Chapman, a barrel-chested
beast of a man who goes by the nickname "Dog"
and looks like he just climbed out of a professional-
wrestling ring. He sports a teased blond mullet that
flows down past his shoulders, wraparound Oakley
sunglasses, spray-tanned skin, and a giant gold-chain
necklace.

Dog flew in last night from his home in Honolulu,
but he didn't come alone. With him is his wiry twenty-
seven-year-old son, Leland, and Tim, his standoffish
"blood brother"—whatever that means.

He also brought along a film crew: three camera
operators, two field producers, a sound mixer, and a
production assistant.

Min had reached out to this former bail bonds-
man turned bounty hunter after seeing the video he'd
posted online pledging to find Andrew Luster.

Unlike the Feds, Dog took Min's story seriously right
away. He agreed to come to Mexico, locate Luster, and
bring him to justice, but only if Min and Mona partici-
pated in the filming. Dog is hoping to sell a reality-TV
series about his life to an American cable network, and
footage of him capturing one of the richest and most
notorious sex offenders in the world might help make
that Hollywood dream a reality.

Min and Mona were dubious, to put it mildly. But
what other choice did they have?

"So now what?" Mona asks. "We all just sit around
and wait?"

"Pretty much, ma'am," Dog answers. "We'll stay out
of your way as best we can. When Luster shows up,
you all just act natural. Bring him out here to the pool
like last time. Me, Leland, Tim, and the crew—we'll all
be hiding. Over there, there, and there. When the time
is right, we'll jump out and bag him, cameras rolling—
and the Lord willing."

Min can't believe what he's hearing. It's nuts. "What
happens if something goes wrong?" he asks. "What if
David—I mean, Andrew—resists? What if he's carrying a weapon?"

Dog snickers. "A surfer-bro trust-fund kid? I think I
can handle him." He pulls a can of mace from his utility

belt and what looks like a metal flashlight attached to a pistol grip. He presses the trigger. *Buzzzz*. It's a stun gun.

Mona and her husband trade anxious looks. What the hell have they gotten themselves into?

There's no turning back now. Andrew should be arriving in just a few hours.

But he doesn't.

CHAPTER 31

June 18, 2003

ANDREW LUSTER FLUTTERS OPEN his eyes, but he can't see much of anything.

He looks around the small, dark room he's lying in, trying to get his bearings.

He groans and rubs his pounding forehead.

He always forgets. He's getting older; at thirty-nine, he can't drink as much as he used to.

But the fun he had last night was worth it—and the proof is the beautiful naked woman passed out next to him in his bed.

When he'd fled California for Mexico six months ago, Andrew was afraid he'd feel homesick. Unsatisfied. Adrift. He was worried he'd miss his former lifestyle, especially the easy access he had to an unlimited supply of impressionable girls.

But then he ended up in Puerto Vallarta, a party town that makes Santa Barbara look like a retirement village.

Its waves are bigger. Its bars stay open later. And its women—American spring-breakers and locals alike—are some of the hottest and wildest he's ever seen.

Andrew might be a wanted felon, but, ironically, he's never felt freer. He wouldn't go back to the U.S. now even if he could.

"Hey, *chica*. Wake up. *Despierta*."

He nudges the snoring young Mexican woman with smooth, hazelnut-hued flesh who's wrapped up in the white bedsheets.

When all she does is grumble, Andrew, completely naked, gets out of bed and throws open the curtains. Midday sunlight floods in, illuminating the rows of empty liquor bottles and heaps of dirty clothing strewn about his cramped, dingy motel room.

It's not the Four Seasons, but it sure as hell beats prison.

Andrew traipses across the ugly shag carpeting to the dresser. He picks up a half-smoked joint, lights it, and takes a drag just as his room phone rings.

"*¿Bueno?*"

"David! Min Labanauskas here. Glad I caught you. Thought you might be away from your desk having lunch or something."

Andrew glances at the dusty clock-radio on his night-stand: 1:08 p.m. "Nope. Working hard. What's up?"

"Why don't you tell *me*? You've stood us up every day this week."

"Yeah. Sorry about that. Things at the office have been a little crazy."

"Hey, I get it. You're a busy guy. But, listen, those units I told you about? I might have some outside interest. Which is great news. But I still want them to go to *you*. I can go as low as sixty-five."

"The thing is, Min, I've been thinking—"

"Fine—sixty. Final offer."

Andrew takes another puff of pot. For a while, he *was* considering parking some cash in a real estate venture down here. But the more he thought about it, the riskier it seemed. Too much of a paper trail. Besides, Andrew wants to stay liquid—and mobile—in case he has to make a run for it again. "I appreciate the offer, man. I really do. I just don't think it's for me anymore."

"Hmm. I've got an idea. Remind me, where are you staying these days?"

"I'm in Puerto Vallarta. Got a nice little room at the Motel Los Angeles."

"I'm sure it's lovely. But I betcha it's nothing compared to Costa Custodio."

Andrew grunts. That's an understatement.

"Come back and spend a few more nights with us. Remember why you loved this place so much. If you're still not interested after that, I'll never mention it again. Promise."

Andrew rubs his eyes. This Min guy just won't leave him alone.

He takes a final drag on his joint, now burned down to a nub, and drops it into an empty Corona bottle.

When Andrew looks up, he sees that the beautiful Mexican girl he brought home last night is awake and sitting up in bed. She's staring at him, smiling seductively. She beckons him over with her finger, then slips that finger between her legs.

"Sorry, Min. I gotta go."

CHAPTER 32

AROUND NINE O'CLOCK THAT evening, Andrew starts to get hungry. His hangover has more or less worn off, and he wants to put some food in his belly before he fills it up later with more booze.

He's got a hankering for beef tacos, and the best ones around here come from a tiny stand on Calle Honduras, just off the beach, about a mile away. He could walk, but he decides to drive. After showering and slipping into the cleanest shirt he can find on his floor, Andrew hops into the beat-up silver Dodge Dart he recently bought for a few hundred dollars and heads out.

He turns onto one of the busy main roads through the city and rolls down his window. The rush of the breeze is cool and invigorating.

Andrew glances in his rearview and notices a gray Buick sedan cruising a few car lengths behind him. He doesn't think much of it. But after a few blocks, when Andrew turns left down a side street, the Buick does too.

Strange.

Just to prove to himself that he's being paranoid, Andrew makes another left turn, heading back in the direction he came.

Again, so does the Buick.

Okay, *now* his suspicions are raised. His senses are on high alert.

Andrew tries to make out the plates, but it's too dark to get a good look. He can't see the driver either. Is it the U.S. Marshals? The FBI? The Mexican *federales*?

How the hell did they find me?

Doesn't matter. Andrew's only goal right now is to get away without drawing too much attention or causing a scene.

Thinking fast, he decides to see what the pursuit vehicle does when he throws it a curveball.

First, he turns back onto the busy main road, going in the opposite direction.

Sure enough, the Buick stays on his tail like a shark silently stalking its prey.

Two blocks later, Andrew makes his move. Without signaling, he cuts the wheel hard to the right and slams on his brakes. Other cars honk furiously as he comes to a screeching stop on the shoulder of the road.

To Andrew's surprise, the Buick keeps on driving.

It passes him, and he sees a middle-aged woman in

the driver's seat and two giggly little girls in back before it disappears down the road.

Andrew exhales. False alarm.

Feeling a little foolish, he pulls back into traffic and resumes his trip. Minutes later, he parks his car down the street from the taco stand, walks over, and gets in line.

There's a decent-size crowd of both locals and tourists milling around on the beach and the promenade, their voices and laughter wafting through the warm night air. Andrew looks out at the ocean, shimmering in the moonlight. Still feeling on edge from earlier, he shuts his eyes, trying to hear the calming sound of the waves over the din of the street.

Suddenly, he hears something else.

Squealing tires.

Slamming doors.

Andrew turns and opens his eyes.

A brawny giant with a flowing blond mane is charging right at him.

So are about six other men, some of whom are holding...video cameras?

Andrew barely has time to register this bizarre scene before the blond man grabs him around his waist and tackles him to the ground.

"Andrew Stuart Luster," the man screams, "you're under arrest in the name of the United States government and Mexico!"

Before Andrew can respond, he feels several more people pounce on him and roughly cuff his hands behind his back. Then multiple pairs of arms scoop him up and start hauling him away.

"Stop!" he screams. "*¡Déjame!* I'm being kidnapped! Help! *¡Ayuda, ayuda!*"

But it's no use.

Andrew is dragged—thrashing and kicking, writhing and screaming—across the pavement and thrown into the back of a black SUV.

It peels off into the night.

CHAPTER 33

HANDCUFFED, BLINDFOLDED, ABDUCTED—
Andrew has never been more terrified in his entire life.

He can feel himself being bumped and jostled as the SUV speeds along Puerto Vallarta's potholed streets. But he has no idea who's taken him, where they're heading, or what they're going to do with him next.

"We still rolling?" says the man who tackled him. "Okay, good." The man clears his throat. "Now, what you all just witnessed out there is called a dynamic takedown. It's one of my favorite techniques for neutralizing and apprehending a dangerous fugitive. It can be risky in a public place like that but—"

"Fugitive?" Andrew exclaims. "Me? You got the wrong guy!"

"Shut up!" the man roars. He gives Andrew a hard shove for good measure. "I'll tell you when it's your turn to talk. Now, let's try this again. Take two. Folks, what you just witnessed is called a dynamic takedown. It's one of my—"

"What the hell *is* this?" Andrew demands. "Are you filming some kind of movie?"

The man grabs Andrew by the scruff of his neck and pulls him close. "This ain't one of your little nudie flicks, brah, if that's what you're asking. My name's Dog. I'm a bounty hunter. I'm not just bringing your ass back to jail, thank the Lord. I'm making mine famous. I'm gonna be on TV! Maybe you can watch me from your cell."

Andrew is stunned. He wasn't caught by the Feds or by Interpol or even by a private eye. He was captured by a wannabe reality-TV star.

From the front of the van, he hears a man shout, "Damn it—cops!"

From behind, he hears a symphony of approaching sirens.

Normally that sound would fill Andrew with dread. But right now, he feels something much closer to relief.

"Shit!" Dog roars. "Okay, okay. Everybody be cool. Leland, pull over. And whatever happens, you boys keep your cameras rolling! Hear me?"

Andrew feels the SUV slow down and stop.

He hears a small army of Mexican *federales* outside, angrily yelling over one another in Spanish.

He hears Dog and the rest of his team open their doors and get out, then more yelling outside, followed by the familiar metallic *click* and *clack* of handcuffs being slapped onto wrists.

"*Señor, ¿estás bien?*" says one of the officers as he approaches the SUV.

"*¡Sí, gracias!*" Andrew answers. He tries desperately, in broken Spanish, to explain that his name is David Carrera, that he was kidnapped against his will, that all of this is just one big misunderstanding, that he should be released at once.

No such luck.

About twenty minutes later, Andrew, Dog, and the others are all loaded into the back of a police pickup truck and carted away.

CHAPTER 34

ANDREW LUSTER IS THROWN into a small, damp, filthy Puerto Vallarta jail cell.

It's worse than hell because Dog the bounty hunter and the rest of his team are thrown in there with him.

A Mexican police officer is posted outside to keep an eye on the motley group of prisoners, but Andrew doesn't let his guard down for a second. He knows Dog is furious about how things turned out and that he might possibly take it out on him with his fists.

For starters, Dog's reality-TV-show footage was ruined. Worse, he and his crew might be facing criminal charges themselves. In Mexico, bounty hunting is illegal, full stop. And since Dog and his team were acting on their own and broke local laws in the process of apprehending him, they probably won't be entitled to a penny of Andrew's forfeited bail money.

"Tough luck," Andrew sneers when he overhears

Dog and some of the others discussing it. "Maybe you should've minded your own business."

Dog glares at Andrew, steaming. "Maybe you shouldn't have drugged and raped all those women, you prick. If putting you behind bars for the rest of your life means I gotta do a little time myself, that's okay by me."

But Dog and the others don't have to do much time at all. They're released the following afternoon, thanks to the hard work of their excellent lawyer.

Andrew tries to contact Roger Diamond, his high-priced defense attorney, but Diamond's snooty secretary refuses to put the call through. According to her boss, she says, Andrew is officially no longer a client.

Great.

Andrew is annoyed but not worried. He still has lots of money, and there are plenty of good lawyers out there who will be happy to take it from him.

He's also no legal expert, but he's confident that the battle over his extradition back to the United States will be a long-drawn-out one. It could take months. Maybe a year.

More than enough time for Andrew to bribe a couple of cops and make his escape.

But he never gets the chance.

Just four days after his arrest, Andrew receives a visit from a *fiscal adjunto,* an assistant state prosecutor. She informs Andrew that because he entered Mexico under a false name, David Carrera, he is in the country illegally and thus can be immediately deported.

Andrew is stunned. He implores the prosecutor not to send him back. He offers to pay her a small fortune to let him stay. He pleads. He begs. He breaks down into uncontrollable sobs.

But it's no use.

Some twenty-four hours later, under the armed escort of four Mexico-based FBI agents, he's on a commercial flight bound for LAX.

When they arrive in LA, he is immediately transferred to the custody of waiting Ventura County Sheriff's officials to begin serving his one-hundred-and-twenty-four-year sentence.

After nearly four decades, Andrew Luster has finally run out of luck.

EPILOGUE

April 2013. Ten Years Later

TONJA BALDEN PULLS ANOTHER Kleenex from the travel pack she keeps in her purse and blots her red, wet eyes.

She's sitting cross-legged on a beach towel staring out at the ocean, searching the waves for some kind of solace. Her husband, Jon, has his arm wrapped around her. Lisa is holding her hand.

"It . . . it . . . it's just not fair," she says. "How could the judge do that?"

"I know, honey," says Jon. "It's not. But fifty years is still a really long time."

"He was supposed to *die* in there! Now he's going to get *out?*"

"When he's *eighty-nine*," Lisa stresses gently. "There's a very good chance—"

"What about parole? Good behavior? *Another* appeal? An even *better* lawyer?" Tonja balls the tissue in her fist.

"That son of a bitch could be released *decades* earlier than that, and both of you know it!"

The three sit in silence for a moment, listening to the lapping water.

All morning they've been trying to process the shocking news. Because the original judge presiding over Andrew Luster's trial didn't properly follow state law, which requires that specific reasons be given for ordering multiple sentences to be served consecutively, Andrew's new attorney was able to convince an appeals judge that his sentences should be served *concurrently.* This had the effect of shortening Andrew's overall sentence from a hundred and twenty-four years to just fifty.

Jon's right, of course. That's still a very long time.

But to Tonja, it feels like a slap in the face. It's dredged up all the pain and anguish she felt over a decade ago, when she bravely testified at Andrew's trial, and two years before that, when she first watched the video of her own rape. And four years before *that,* when she and Jon were the targets of Andrew's stalking, harassment, and death threats.

Tonja has worked hard to put those awful experiences behind her. To process and move past the trauma and get on with her life. But every few years, it seems, something happens to drag her back.

When, she wonders, *will this nightmare end?*

"Mom! Dad! Aunt Lisa! Look what I can do!" Tonja

and Jon's twelve-year-old daughter calls to them from the ocean's edge. She's a bright and bubbly girl, outgoing and self-confident.

Tonja puts on a smile. "Show me, baby!"

Her daughter does a string of cartwheels, ending with a backward knee tuck.

Tonja, Jon, and Lisa all shout, "Bravo! Wow! Great job!" Their little gymnast takes a theatrical bow, then scurries back into the water.

Watching her daughter always fills Tonja with joy, pride, and love. But today, her heart and mind can only dwell in darkness.

She wonders how many other women out there Andrew might have drugged, raped, and filmed. Women whose stories will never be known. Women who will never see justice served.

Tonja worries about how many other *Andrews* are out there. Smart, charming, handsome, wealthy men who have committed the same crimes—or even worse ones.

How can she ever feel truly safe again in this world?

How can she ever keep her *daughter* safe?

Tonja knows the answer.

She can't.

Because anyone can have a secret dark side—even the people we love.

A
MURDEROUS
AFFAIR

JAMES PATTERSON
WITH ANDREW BOURELLE

PART ONE

CHAPTER 1

Pikeville, Kentucky. May 1987

THE UNMARKED FBI SEDAN cruises through the Kentucky hills, lush and green after a wet spring. Mark Putnam drives with the window rolled down and his elbow propped on the frame. Neil Whittaker, a state trooper, rides shotgun. Mark is wearing a suit; Whittaker is in his uniform.

When Mark arrived in Pikeville three months earlier, one of the first things he did was join the local cops on ride-alongs so he could learn the lay of the land and earn the respect of the men he'd be working closely with. Today's journey, however, has a different purpose. Trooper Whittaker is taking Mark out to meet a potential informant.

"Now, one thing about Susan," Whittaker says, raising his voice to be heard over the wind rushing past the windows, "she's got a reputation for telling some tall tales, and you can't always be sure if what she's saying is the actual truth or something she just wishes were true."

Mark frowns. "Sounds great," he says sarcastically. "Just what I look for in an informant."

Mark likes Whittaker; they have a good rapport. If they didn't, he wouldn't joke like this with the trooper.

"The thing is," Whittaker says, "she's got a good head on her shoulders. She's smarter than people give her credit for. And everyone likes her. She'll be able to find stuff out for you, and no one will suspect her of a thing."

Mark is skeptical. He's seen the file on the woman. Her name is Susan Daniels Smith. She is twenty-five, has two kids, and lives with her ex-husband, a known drug dealer.

"I'm not sure why they're still living together," Whittaker says. "It might be they filed for divorce just so they could get more welfare money. Or it could be they actually split but Susan has nowhere else to go."

Mark had wanted to tap the ex-husband, Clint, as an informant. Clint's definitely plugged into illegal activity in this region of Kentucky. But Whittaker had cautioned him that Clint, who'd already done hard time for selling drugs, was too unreliable. Whittaker suggested Susan instead, saying they'd grown up together, and he had a high opinion of her. Plus he thought she might be interested in making a little extra money.

Whittaker directs Mark to turn down a gravel road that twists back into the hills. From there, they turn off onto another road, and another, until they are traveling through the woods on what could hardly be called a road—more like two wheel ruts straddling a berm of weeds. Bushes crowd both sides of the lane, the branches clawing the sedan. Finally, the route opens into a grassy clearing with a couple of rusted-out automobile husks that might once have been used as moonshine stills.

Mark and Whittaker step out of the car to wait. The wild grass in the clearing is two feet high, and grasshoppers jump from stalk to stalk. The air is loud with insects and birds. They hear the long, low honk of a semi in the distance, probably a coal truck leaving a mine. Mark closes his eyes and tries to enjoy the sound of the insects and the warmth of the sun on his face.

"Here she comes," Whittaker says.

A car, an old maroon-and-green Chevy Nova that looks pieced together from two cars, pulls into the clearing, its engine chugging loudly. The woman behind the wheel spots Mark and smiles. Her expression says, *What's someone as handsome as this fella doing in a town like ours?*

Mark gives her a slight smile in return. He's a little surprised himself; when he'd learned his new potential informant had two kids and was married to—or at least living with—a drug dealer, he'd made a few assumptions about her appearance: she'd probably look much older than her years and be either overweight or grossly malnourished with listless stringy hair, acne-scarred skin, and a mouth full of rotten yellow teeth.

Susan Daniels Smith looks nothing like that. Her teeth are straight and white, her hair shiny and healthy, her skin glowing and unblemished. She opens the door and strolls over to them; she's wearing tight jeans, a black tank top showing off slim arms, and a small gold necklace that lies against her tan skin. She looks like a carefree college senior on a campus in the South, not a mother of two who never finished the seventh grade.

"Howdy, y'all," she says with a charming Southern twang. "Let's make this quick. Clint thinks I borrowed the car to get the welfare check. I can't take all day."

Whittaker makes the introductions, and Susan extends her hand to Mark in a businesslike gesture. "Nice to meet you," she says, pronouncing the last two words as one—*meet'cha.*

Susan's hand feels soft and small in Mark's strong weight-lifter's grip. "The pleasure's mine," Mark says.

CHAPTER 2

SUSAN CRUISES DOWN THE road, singing along to a Juice Newton song on the radio. The green trees blur by, and Susan reaches her arm out the window and moves her hand in the wind like it's a bird.

She's in a good mood.

It's a beautiful day, she has a moment to herself for once, and she has her welfare check in her pocket—one of them, anyway. Like a lot of people in the area, she double-dips by collecting checks from both Kentucky and West Virginia.

Being able to buy groceries is one reason she's in a good mood, but mostly she's feeling positive about her meeting with Neil Whittaker and that FBI agent. She played tough with him, saying that she wasn't sure she wanted to work for the Bureau because she'd had a cousin who'd been an informant and gotten stiffed on his payment.

But the truth is, she's excited.

Not just about the money. That's a big part of it, but she's also eager to do something that might be meaningful. She feels stuck in this dead-end town, living week to week—sometimes day to day—on government checks and whatever money her ex throws her.

She wants something more from life, and maybe this is the way to get it.

Also, it doesn't hurt that this Mark Putnam fellow is cute. She was bummed when she noticed his wedding ring.

As she approaches the trailer she and the kids share with Clint, she slows down. She isn't ready to go back. Tucked deep in the woods, the trailer was once a baby-blue color, but now, with all the paint flaking off, it's an ashen gray. There's not enough room inside, and there's no garage, of course, so the stuff a normal family would store indoors is stacked up outside against one wall— toolboxes, coolers, and cardboard boxes that are sagging in on themselves and coming apart at the seams after sitting out in the weather too long. There's a firepit out front with a handful of plastic lawn chairs around it. The grass is overgrown except for a dirt track the kids have made with their bikes and Big Wheels.

As she pulls up out front, Clint bangs open the screen door and trudges her way, wearing jeans with holes in the knees and a Hank Williams Jr. shirt over his wiry frame. In his hand is a wrinkled paper grocery bag with the top folded over; it looks like he's carrying a large sack lunch.

Of course there isn't any food in the bag.

"What took you so damn long?" he says before she even has the car in park.

"Don't get your panties in a wad," Susan tells him. "Where you gotta go in such a hurry?"

"Making my rounds," he says, snatching the keys from her.

From inside the house, she can hear their younger child, two-year-old Alex, crying.

As Clint fires up the engine, he calls out the window to Susan, "We've got friends coming to stay with us for a few days. Make them feel welcome."

"Who?" Susan says.

Clint doesn't answer; he steps on the gas and roars down the road, kicking up gravel.

When Susan enters the trailer, Alex rushes into her arms. She lifts him and pats his head, and immediately his cries subside. Five-year-old Samantha is in the living room watching some daytime talk show that's way too adult for her.

Even though Susan cleaned the place this morning, it's already a mess. On the kitchen table are half a dozen empty beer bottles and dirty dishes with the remnants of the kids' lunches sitting half eaten, collecting flies. Ziploc bags are strewn about, some with a powdery residue of something inside. The floor is cluttered with the children's toys.

Susan takes a deep breath. Apparently, cleaning up after everyone else has become her lot in life.

She lets the kids watch TV while she picks up their toys and does the dishes. As she's putting the last plate in the drying rack, a car rumbles up to the trailer. She can tell just from the sound of the engine that it's not her husband's Nova.

She looks out the screen door to see a Pontiac Firebird Trans Am. Paul Collins—who everyone calls Cat Eyes—climbs out of the driver's side, and his girl-friend, Crystal Black, steps out of the passenger side, adjusting a skirt that leaves little to the imagination.

These two visitors are the exact people Susan was afraid Clint meant.

"Hey, good-looking," Cat Eyes calls to Susan as he walks through the overgrown lawn, a duffel bag slung over his shoulder. "You like my car? It's just like the one from *Smokey and the Bandit*."

"If you can afford to make payments on that," Susan says, coming out onto the front steps and drying her hands with a dishrag, "what do you need to stay with us for?"

She delivers the words in a playful, teasing tone, but she intends them to have a little bite.

"Don't worry," he says, stretching his arms out for a hug. "It won't be for long. I've got plans."

He wraps her up and lifts her off her feet, and she forces an uncomfortable laugh. He smells like he hasn't showered in a week. One of his hands cups her butt and gives it a squeeze. She smacks his arm and twists out of his grip. Crystal is eyeing them without a hint of good humor.

Cat Eyes holds Susan by the shoulders and stares at her like she's a trophy he's wanted to win his whole life. "How's the prettiest girl in Pike County?" Cat Eyes says, apparently not caring that his girlfriend is standing only a few feet from them.

Susan wants to squirm away, but she holds his intense gaze. He gets his nickname from his eyes, which have bright emerald-green irises that look more feline than human. A lot of women have fallen for those eyes, but not Susan. She knows Paul "Cat Eyes" Collins too well, and to her, his eyes don't look seductive.

They look cold. Calculating. Predatory.

"Come on in," Susan says, forcing a smile. "My house is your house."

CHAPTER 3

KATHY PUTNAM STANDS BY the stove, stirring a pot of spaghetti sauce with a wooden spoon. Her and Mark's two-year-old daughter, Jenny, is on the floor playing with Barbie dolls. Kathy tastes the sauce. She's starving.

She's eating for two now, after all.

The pregnancy is just starting to show, but already she has a ravenous appetite. She hopes Mark will be back soon. He came home about an hour ago, quickly changed into his running clothes, promised to be back in time for supper, and headed out. She doesn't know where he gets his energy. He lifted weights in the garage before going to work at seven a.m., and still that wasn't enough; he had to get a run in before the sun went down. Maybe he needs to work off the anxiety brought on by his stressful job.

It can't be easy being a rookie FBI agent in a brand-new town.

They arrived in Pikeville in February, and since Mark has no office assistant, no one to help him, Kathy has been filling that role, taking messages for him at home, relaying information to various contacts, and sometimes typing his reports.

The cordless phone on the counter rings, and Kathy answers it, tucking it into the crook of her neck so she can keep stirring.

"Is Mr. Putnam there?" asks a female voice. She sounds young but confident, not the least bit timid.

"He went out for a run," Kathy says. "He should be back soon. May I take a message?"

The person on the other end is quiet for a moment, as if she's thinking. "No," she finally says, some of the confidence gone from her tone. "That's okay."

"May I tell him who called?"

"No. I'll call back."

"Hang on," Kathy says, "this might be him now."

Mark walks into the kitchen, his forehead beaded with sweat. He strips off his soaked T-shirt and stands before Kathy shirtless, moisture glistening on his muscles.

Kathy cups her hand over the receiver so the woman on the other end can't hear. "For you," she says. "A woman. Won't give her name."

Mark takes the phone. "Mark Putnam speaking," he says. "Oh, hi, Susan."

As he talks, Mark kneels and kisses Jenny's forehead. Then he takes his wet T-shirt and wipes his brow with it. Kathy listens to his half of the conversation. She hears something about cat eyes, which she doesn't understand, and something about bank robberies, which sounds intriguing.

"That was my wife who answered," Mark says to the woman. "Her name's Kathy. If you ever need to leave a message for me, you can do it through her."

Kathy has enjoyed being Mark's unofficial secretary. Working, even informally, for the FBI has been a welcome addition to days otherwise filled with cooking, doing laundry, and attempting to potty-train Jenny— which has thus far been an exercise in frustration.

When Mark hangs up the phone, he claps his hands together with excitement. "Got a fantastic lead," he says.

As they sit at the table and eat, Mark explains that before they arrived in Pikeville, there had been a series of bank robberies throughout the tri-corner area. Hundreds of thousands of dollars had been stolen from small-town banks in the Appalachian Mountains of Kentucky, West Virginia, and Virginia. The FBI suspected a guy named Paul "Cat Eyes" Collins, but they didn't know where to find him.

"He went to prison for seven years for bank robbery," Mark says. "And sure enough, this most recent string of robberies started right around the time he was released."

Mark says that his new informant claims that Cat

Eyes and his girlfriend, Crystal Black, are going to be staying with her for a while.

"Their names are really Cat Eyes and Crystal Black?" Kathy says in disbelief. "They sound like characters in a bad movie."

Mark laughs. "No kidding. And apparently this guy idolizes Burt Reynolds. Susan said he showed up today in a Firebird like the one in *Smokey and the Bandit*."

Kathy rolls her eyes. She tries not to be judgmental about the people in the community, but there's no doubt that Pikeville, Kentucky, is far different from New Haven, Connecticut, where they came from. Located deep in the Appalachian hills, Pikeville is a good two-hour drive to Huntington, West Virginia, and another hour farther than that to Lexington, Kentucky. Pikeville is surrounded by other dot-on-the-map towns tucked into the mountains, with dirt-road hollows—or hollers, as the locals call them—splitting off into the hills. With the coal-mining industry suffering, the region has one of the highest poverty rates in the country and one of the lowest high-school-graduation rates. Drug use is rampant. Much of the criminal activity in the area is associated with drugs, from dealers pushing their products to addicts breaking laws to make quick cash to pay for their next fix.

Kathy was wary when Mark received the news that he'd be heading to a sleeper office in Kentucky that no one seemed to care about. Pikeville seemed like the kind of place careers went to die, not begin. But Mark told her that the assignment was a good thing.

"They don't expect much out of that office," Mark said. "That means if I do a good job, they'll really take notice."

They moved to Pikeville, and it turned out that Mark liked the area a lot. He poured himself into his work during the day, went for runs in the evening, and fell asleep with case files spread out around him in their bed. He hadn't made any close friends yet, but he was so busy he didn't seem to care.

It was Kathy who'd been lonely these past few months, sitting at home with Jenny all day and hoping for phone calls from Mark's contacts to relieve her boredom.

"What's this Susan like?" Kathy asks, not expecting much from a woman who is apparently friends with bank robbers.

"You'd like her," Mark says, taking a bite of spaghetti. He says that Susan is a high-school dropout, like half the population in the tri-corner area, and lives with her two kids and her ex-husband, a known drug dealer. "But she's got a lot of moxie. If she had been born in different circumstances," he says, "I think she could have really made something of her life."

"Will I get to meet her?" Kathy says.

"I hope so," Mark says. "I think you two would hit it off."

CHAPTER 4

THE FBI OFFICE IN Pikeville, Kentucky, consists of a single small room in the federal courthouse building. There are two desks, each with its own filing cabinet, and a single window looking out over the town. The brick walls are adorned with maps of the three states that converge on the tri-corner area—road maps, topographic maps, and detailed city maps of all the small municipalities hidden in the Appalachian hills. There's a small table, a fax machine, a paper shredder, and a coffeemaker.

Mark sits in a square of sunlight at one of the desks waiting for a call back from his supervisor at the Covington office.

The other desk sits empty.

When Mark arrived in Pikeville, the other agent, Jack Cornell, was just days away from transferring to Lexington. He took Mark to lunch at one of the few restaurants in town and gave him a quick rundown of the territory and a warning about what Mark had gotten himself into.

"You're a Yankee in the mountains of Appalachia," he said. "This place will chew you up and spit you out if you ain't careful."

Cornell was concerned about Mark being solo and not having a proper mentor. He said that Mark would be better off in a bigger office, with more agents around to show him the ropes. Apparently, whoever assigned Mark to this office thought he'd been a Connecticut state trooper before joining the FBI, someone with ample law enforcement experience. But that wasn't the case—Mark was a rookie fresh out of the FBI Academy who'd previously worked only as a clerk for the FBI, not an agent.

But once the mistake was discovered, the Bureau didn't want to pull Mark out. And Mark didn't want to go. He was ready, he assured Cornell.

"You ever have any questions about anything," Jack Cornell said, "you call up to Covington and ask, you hear me? You're not out here on your own."

Mark promised, and he'd kept that promise. He was in regular communication with his superiors. He wanted to make a name for himself in Pikeville; he didn't want to cut any corners or do anything wrong.

The phone rings—the call Mark has been waiting for. Mark tells Supervisory Special Agent Trent Cavanagh that he'd like to pay a new informant. "She claims she had a relative who was an informant who never got paid," he says. "I'd like to give her some good-faith money to show that this is for real."

Mark asks for five hundred dollars, nervous that his supervisor will balk at the amount.

"Why so little?" Cavanagh says.

"Um, well, she hasn't done anything yet," Mark says, surprised.

"Listen," Cavanagh says, "we've got deep pockets when it comes to paying informants. There's money at your disposal, understand?"

When Mark hangs up the phone, he's relieved.

He's also excited to share the news with Susan. He'd meant what he said to Kathy last night about how Susan might have done something with her life if she'd been born into different circumstances. Maybe the FBI can help her get out of a bad position and make some improvements in her living situation.

And maybe Susan can give Mark information that will break open some cases for him.

Maybe the two of them will be good for each other.

CHAPTER 5

I CAN'T SLEEP, MOMMY. It's too noisy."

"I'm sorry, honey," Susan tells Samantha, adjusting her covers. "I'll tell them to keep it down."

In the living area next to where the kids and Susan share a bed, Clint and Cat Eyes are talking loudly over a radio blaring Lynyrd Skynyrd. Susan walks into the cigarette-smoke-filled room and turns the radio down, then says, "The kids are trying to sleep. Why don't y'all head out to a bar or something? At least go sit outside."

"We'll leave soon," Clint says, opening the refrigerator door and pulling out three bottles of beer. "After we drink these."

Before Susan can object, Clint twists the top off the first one and hands it to Cat Eyes. The second he gives to Crystal, who's sitting on the couch next to her boyfriend. The third he swigs himself.

The table is filled with empty bottles and overflowing ashtrays. Cat Eyes has tapped out four lines of cocaine onto a magazine cover. "You want to do the first line?" he says to Susan, holding a straw out.

She considers it but declines. As much as she'd love a good temporary escape from her reality, she has bigger goals on her mind these days.

Cat Eyes snorts two lines and then sits back on the couch, rubbing his nose and blinking his watery eyes. Susan thinks now might be a good time to ask some questions.

"So tell me," she says, sitting down on the couch with Cat Eyes and Crystal, "what are these big plans of yours?"

"Banks," he says with a smile, shifting so his leg touches Susan's.

Crystal eyes them both reproachfully, but Susan ignores her.

"Not banks again, Paul," Susan says playfully. "Didn't you do enough time for that already?"

"It's the only thing I know," he says. "It's the only thing I was ever good at."

If you're so good at it, Susan thinks, *how come you got caught?* "What do you do when you rob a bank?" she asks. "How is it done?"

Cat Eyes laughs at the question. "What, you gonna start robbing banks?"

"Maybe," she says, smiling at Cat Eyes, then giving

Clint a hard stare. "I've gotta get out of this dump somehow."

Cat Eyes and Clint laugh as if this is the funniest thing they've ever heard. Clint takes a break from laughing to snort a line.

"Okay, little Susie," Cat Eyes says, leaning over to grab his duffel bag. "I'll teach you." He unzips it and reaches his hand inside. "First thing you need is one of these." He holds up a black ski mask, then roots farther down in the duffel bag. "And one of these!" he announces.

He holds up a single-shot twelve-gauge shotgun whose stock and barrel have been cut off. The whole thing isn't more than about a foot and a half long and it fits in Cat Eyes's hand like some kind of large dueling pistol.

"Is it loaded?" Susan asks, trying to keep the tremor out of her voice. That duffel bag has been sitting on the floor for days and her children have walked by it and played around it. Alex even crawled on top of the duffel bag earlier today, treating it like a beanbag chair.

"Of course it is," Cat Eyes says, breaking the gun to reveal the double-aught buckshot shell inside. "What good is a gun if you can't shoot nobody with it?"

CHAPTER 6

SUSAN WALKS THROUGH A path in the forest. The sun is low, casting long shadows across the grass and giving the woods an eerie look. It's silent; the birds and insects have quieted for the day. Susan nears a spot where the roads intersect and then stands back out of sight. She doesn't want anyone driving by to see her.

A car approaches, its headlights off even though it's getting darker by the minute. When Mark's sedan rolls to a stop on the gravel shoulder, Susan emerges from where she's been hiding as if all of this is completely normal. She opens the passenger door and jumps in, feeling an electric excitement. It reminds her of sneaking off with boys when she was a teenager, drinking and making out on back roads, or of when she ran off with Clint, knowing he was going to be trouble but unable to stop herself.

"I don't want to talk here," she says to Mark. "Just drive somewhere. Anywhere."

Mark drives, saying nothing. Susan looks at his strong hands on the wheel, his cool demeanor as he navigates through the hills. Dusk is giving way to night, and he switches on the headlights. He finds a remote back road and pulls the car over next to a ravine. They're behind a coal mine and can see the glow of lights from over the ridge.

"You got something for me?" Susan asks, giddy.

"First, I want to get something straight," he says. "You've got a reputation for exaggerating, making stuff up. If you're going to be an informant for the FBI, I need to be able to trust what you tell me."

Susan rolls her eyes. "Pike County is about as boring as it gets," she says. "Girl's gotta do something to keep life interesting. I just make up fun stuff, nothing that would hurt no one."

For example, she says, one time she told everyone she used to have a pet parrot named Paco but Clint made her get rid of it because it would listen to Clint on the phone and repeat what he said. It would squawk, *Where's my money?* and *How much for a kilo?*

"I told people I let it go and it flew off through the woods. 'It's out there somewhere,' I'd say, 'a beautiful bird with amazing colors that has no business in the woods of Kentucky.' None of it was true. We never had no bird. It was just a nice story."

At heart, Susan lied so she could see her life the way

she wanted it to be instead of the way it was. She'd tried to convince Clint to get a parrot, but he'd dismissed the idea outright, so she'd made up a story where she actually got what she wanted.

"Okay, but listen, Susan. This is important. When it comes to us," Mark says, pointing back and forth between himself and Susan, "I need to trust you. That's the only way this will work. I need your word that you'll be truthful."

Susan is moved by his sincerity. Most people didn't care if she was telling the truth because they didn't really care what she had to say. It was a nice change to have someone want correct and reliable information from her.

"I can do that," she says earnestly, then adds with a grin, "The whole truth and nothing but the truth."

Mark pulls an envelope from his jacket pocket. "There's five hundred dollars in here," he says. "It's good-faith money to let you know we'll pay you for information. There's more where this came from if your tips lead to any arrests."

Susan reaches out to take the envelope, but Mark doesn't let go yet. He fixes her with a serious stare, discernible even in the shadows.

"If you take this," he says, "you will be a paid FBI informant. It's official. No turning back. Are you ready for this?"

Susan grins and snatches the envelope from him. "You bet your ass I am."

CHAPTER 7

August 1987

PUTNAM RESIDENCE," KATHY SAYS, tucking the phone between her ear and her shoulder so she can continue wiping down the kitchen counter.

"Hi, Kathy. It's Susan."

"Oh, hi!" Kathy says, excited to have someone to talk to.

It's been over two months since Susan became Mark's informant, and she and Kathy have struck up a friendship. Although they haven't actually met in person, they've become telephone buddies, spending time almost every day talking. Susan seemed hesitant at first to talk to Kathy, but Kathy quickly put her at ease by asking questions about her children. Susan is a few years younger than Kathy, but her children are older, and Kathy is worried about having two to contend with and welcomes any advice.

Since that first conversation, Susan calls almost daily,

usually to pass an update on to Mark but often for no official reason at all, just to chat with Kathy.

"Can you talk?" Susan asks.

"Sure, Jenny is napping," Kathy says, sitting at the kitchen table. "How's it going?"

"I'm just tired of these houseguests," Susan says. "They're eating my food, watching my TV. I tell you what—the life of a bank robber ain't all that glamorous. Not when you spend all the money on cars and drugs and end up mooching off friends."

The information Susan has given Mark has been helpful—and it will be even more helpful if she agrees to testify about it in court at some point in the future—but for now Mark doesn't have enough to make an arrest, which means Susan is stuck with her two unwanted houseguests for a while longer.

Kathy feels sorry about what Susan endures day to day. It's bad enough living with an unreliable drug dealer, but now she also has to live with a bank robber who hits on her constantly, despite the disapproving stares of his girlfriend. And to top it all off, Susan's trying to raise two children in that environment.

"I love my kids," Susan says, "but I curse the day I ever met Clint."

Susan had had big dreams of finishing high school, but she didn't even make it *to* high school. Growing up an honest-to-God coal miner's daughter, Susan had eight brothers and sisters living in a home not much bigger than the trailer she lives in now. When her father was out of work, which was often, the family subsisted on welfare.

One day a handsome man drove by on a motorcycle, stopped, and whistled at her. She climbed on the back, and that was it—she was Clint's girl. She was fifteen; he was twenty-two.

She went to live with him in his trailer and helped him with his business affairs. She was smart and could keep track of names, dates, dollar amounts. She smoked pot but mostly kept clear of the harder stuff.

"When he went to prison, I thought about leaving," she says. "But he promised me when he got out, he'd go straight. No more dealing. At first, he kept his word, so I married him. I thought we had a different kind of life ahead of us. Maybe it would be hard, but it would be lawful, and that felt good."

The honeymoon glow didn't last long. Clint hurt his back at work, but his disability claim was rejected, so he went back to selling drugs.

"We moved around, went to Chicago. He made some contacts. It was exciting for a while," Susan says. "But then I got pregnant and realized I didn't want this life for my kids."

The two ended up back in Pikeville as the marriage fell apart.

"After we got divorced," she says, "I didn't have nowhere to go. What was I supposed to do? I got no money and no education. So I stayed with Clint and told myself I was doing it for my kids."

As Kathy listens, she looks around the home she shares with Mark. It's no mansion by any stretch of the imagination, but it's nicer than anything they could have bought in Connecticut. Two stories, four bedrooms, two full baths. The cost of living in this part of Kentucky is quite low, and they can afford the mortgage payments without trouble.

During the day, when it's just her and Jenny, the house feels almost too big. Too quiet.

Kathy encourages Susan to use the money from the FBI to get out of Pikeville and start over somewhere new. "Trust me," Kathy says. "I know where you're coming from."

Susan makes a *hmmph* noise, expressing her disbelief that Kathy has any clue what her life is like. Kathy takes a deep breath. She doesn't usually share her story, but she likes Susan and wants to help her. *Mark's right,* Kathy thinks. *Susan will make a good informant. If she can get me to open up about this, she can get anyone to share their secrets.*

"Once you hear what I've been through," Kathy says, "you'll realize my background's not as different from yours as you might think."

"You've got the perfect husband and the perfect life," Susan protests.

"That's true," Kathy says, "but Mark wasn't my first husband."

CHAPTER 8

WHAT?" SUSAN SAYS, GENUINELY surprised. "You're divorced?"

"I got married way too young and to the wrong guy, just like you."

Susan sits on the steps of her trailer, the phone cord stretched out so she can listen to Kathy while keeping an eye on her kids playing out front. Alex is pushing Hot Wheels around in the dirt, and Samantha is imagining conversations between two Barbie dolls, one missing a leg and the other missing her head.

The truth is that when Susan first started talking to Kathy, she didn't *want* to like her. Kathy seemed to have everything Susan longed for, starting with a handsome, reliable husband who put a roof over her head without breaking the law.

But Kathy's interest in Susan's life and her welcoming

manner quickly won Susan over. Mark was business-like; Kathy was personable.

And Kathy, Susan realized, was in need of a friend.

Maybe they were alike in that way.

On the phone, Kathy explains she was directionless in high school and ended up dropping out. She drifted around, making a series of bad decisions and running off with a guy who was trouble—he sounded a lot like Clint. One day, living in South Carolina and trying to scrounge up enough money to return home to her parents, she decided to scam some guys in the military by pretending she had a hotel room full of girls waiting to do anything they wanted. When she ran off without producing what she'd promised, they called the police, who arrested her for prostitution.

"You were arrested for prostitution?" Susan says, but there's no judgment in her voice. When Clint was in prison, she did a lot of things she regrets in order to eat.

The charges were dropped, but Kathy's string of poor choices didn't end there. She met another guy who was bad for her—and ended up marrying that one. He was ten years her senior, and controlling. She'd gotten her GED and was taking classes at the local community college, and he didn't like that.

"One day he beat me up and dumped me in front of my parents' house," Kathy says, her voice trembling on the other end of the phone. "Like he was returning a defective product."

She divorced the guy, earned her associate's degree, found a job as a paralegal. Then she met Mark and life really started to improve.

"Does Mark know about your past?" Susan asks.

"When we were getting serious, I told him. He said he never wanted to talk about it again. Wanted to put it behind us."

"You've got it made now," Susan says, looking with scorn at the trailer she lives in. "You've got yourself a good man to take care of you."

"I take care of him as much as he takes care of me," Kathy says. "We're a team."

Kathy explains that when she met Mark, he had recently graduated from the University of Tampa with a degree in criminology and was working as a night clerk for the FBI in Connecticut. He wanted badly to be an agent, but because of an old shoulder injury, the FBI wouldn't let him enroll in the academy.

"I couldn't believe it," Kathy says. "Mark was in better shape than ninety-nine percent of the agents he clerked for."

"So how did he convince them to let him in?" Susan asks.

"He didn't," Kathy says. "I did." She explains that she called every higher-up in the FBI she could find until she reached someone who would listen to her.

"Like I said, we're a team. That's why I don't mind taking messages for him. I'm sort of like his clerk now, and we're in this together. I wouldn't be where I am without him, that's true. But he wouldn't be where he is without me."

Susan can't help but feel jealous. She and Clint once seemed like a team. She could do that again—be someone's partner in love and in life—if she found the right guy. She'd been young and naive when she'd fallen for Clint. She'd fallen for the bad boy.

Now she wants a good guy.

CHAPTER 9

Elkhorn City, Kentucky. September 1987

PAUL "CAT EYES" COLLINS pulls the black mask over his face as he approaches the back of the bank. His duffel bag, empty except for his shotgun, is slung over his shoulder. He rounds the corner of the building, pushes through the glass double doors, yanks the gun from the bag, and shouts, *"Nobody move or I'll blow your asses to kingdom come!"*

The few patrons inside thrust their hands in the air. Cat Eyes approaches the lone teller working the counter, a good-looking woman in her twenties, and points the pistol-grip shotgun at her freckled face. The nameplate displayed at her station says DEBBIE.

"Got any kids, Debbie?" he says, his words muffled by the mask.

"No," she says, her voice unsteady.

"Want any?"

"Maybe," she says, confused. "Someday."

"If you want to live long enough to have any," he says, dropping the bag on the counter, "you'll fill this up for me."

As she reaches for the duffel bag, he thrusts the gun closer; the sawed-off barrel is only inches from her eyes.

"Don't try anything," he says.

He watches as she opens her drawer and begins dumping in stacks of money. He spins around and surveys the customers, making sure no one has any bright ideas. When Debbie is finished, he tells her to take him to the vault. He follows her into the large walk-in safe. His eyes widen when he sees all the money stacked in neat rows on the stainless-steel shelves.

As the woman kneels to get the bundles off the bottom shelf, Cat Eyes stares at the flesh of her leg showing through a slit in her skirt.

"You're cute," he says. "Want to go out on a date after this is over? I'll take you somewhere nice. I can afford it."

She ignores him.

"Your loss," he mutters. "Bitch."

When the duffel bag is full, Cat Eyes grabs it and heaves it over his shoulder. It's so full, the zipper can't close; the money is nearly spilling out. He wants to laugh, he feels so happy. But he doesn't express any of this to the teller next to him. Instead, he places the barrel of the gun under her chin.

"Don't call the cops for ten minutes, Debbie. If you do, I'll come back here and blow a hole in your head so big, you could drive a car through it. Got it?"

With tears streaming down her cheeks, Debbie nods slightly, the gun below her chin keeping her from moving any more. Cat Eyes heads out the door, walks as fast as he can down the alley behind the bank to where his Trans Am is parked, strips off his mask, and shoves it and the shotgun into the bag.

He opens the passenger door and drops the money onto the seat. But then he hears a loud crack, like a gunshot. He jumps in surprise, and red liquid splatters his chest and face.

Oh, my God! he thinks. *They've shot me.*

Then he realizes it's not blood.

It's ink.

He yanks open the duffel bag. His money and shotgun are dripping with reddish fluid. That teller must have slipped a dye pack into the bag. He spins around and looks back toward the bank; he has half a mind to go in there and teach that teller a lesson. But then the bank alarm goes off, its loud peals ringing through the streets.

Probably every person in town can hear it.

"Shit!" he snaps. He runs around the car, gets into the driver's seat, and jams his foot on the gas pedal; the air fills with rubber smoke. As he barrels out of town, he curses his bad luck. This has never happened to him before.

It's almost as if they knew he was coming.

CHAPTER 10

October 1987

MARK IS SITTING AT his desk typing up a report on Paul Collins's arrest. They found him yesterday hiding out at his mother's house in West Virginia, right where Susan said he would be. The fact that he was caught with a bag of money stained with dye should make the conviction easy.

That and Susan's testimony . . . assuming she'll testify.

As he's writing about Susan's contribution to the arrest, she bursts through the doorway, her face flushed with emotion.

"You shouldn't be here," he says, surprised. "What if someone sees you?"

"I don't give a damn," she says.

"I've got your money," he says, assuming that's why she's barged into his office. "I was going to arrange to bring it to you but I didn't want to call. I know Clint is usually home in the mornings."

"That ain't why I'm here," she says, obviously angry about something. In her hand is the local newspaper, and she slams it down on his desk for him to look at. On the front page is an article about the arrest and a photograph of Mark escorting a handcuffed Cat Eyes across his mother's front lawn, the Trans Am visible in the background.

"Have you seen this?" Susan says, her face red.

He can't imagine what she's angry about. The article didn't mention her in any way—no one will know she's the informant.

"It was a big arrest," he says. "Of course the newspaper is going to cover it."

She leans over the desk—he gets a quick whiff of her perfume—and runs her fingers down the article. Her nails are polished a glossy red.

"There," she says, pointing to a quote from Mark's supervisor, Trent Cavanagh, who came down from Covington for the press conference.

The quote mentions the joint work of the FBI and various law enforcement agencies in the tri-corner area.

"They didn't give you credit at all!" Susan says, her voice cracking with emotion. "You're in the picture but they don't say it's your arrest. This was your case and they don't mention your name once."

"Oh, Susan," he says, "I don't care about having my name in the paper." Mark's touched that Susan's upset on his behalf. *It's sweet,* he thinks, *in a way.* "Listen," he says, taking her hand and directing her to the chair at the other desk, "my superiors are tickled pink with me right now. *They* know I'm the one who put this together. I might not be getting credit in the public eye, but I sure am in the eyes of the agency. That's where it matters to me."

"I just think it's ridiculous you don't get your name in the paper," Susan says, crossing her arms.

Mark dismisses the notion with a wave of his hand. "What's in the paper doesn't usually tell the whole story," he says. "The truth is, *you're* the one who deserves the credit. My supervisors are grateful for your help, and they wanted me to tell you that." This finally puts a smile on her face. "We make a good team," Mark says, which makes her smile grow bigger.

Mark is glad to have relieved the tension in the room. He likes Susan. She's different from any woman he's ever known; she says what's on her mind, she wears her heart on her sleeve, and there's a hint of flirtation in just about everything she says to him.

Mark knows they can't talk all day—although Susan has settled into the seat and looks like she's ready to do just that—so he opens his desk drawer and pulls out the envelope he'd set aside for her. "Here you go. Fifteen hundred dollars. As promised."

She rises from her seat, her demeanor changing again. "No," she says. "You keep it. You didn't get credit in the newspaper. You should have this."

He frowns as he holds out the envelope for her. Susan makes no move to take the money. "This money is for you, Susan."

"I'm not taking it," she says. "You deserve it."

She raises her hands in a gesture that communicates there's no way she's touching the envelope. As she backs out the door, she gives him a wink.

"See you later, partner," she says, and then she's gone.

CHAPTER 11

Freeburn, Kentucky. December 1987

MOLLY DAVIDSON PUSHES A snow shovel along the path to her house. Her gloved hands ache from clearing the driveway. As she tosses the last shovelful of snow onto the pile, she spots a familiar car—a maroon-and-green Nova—slip-sliding its way up the road. It pulls into her driveway, and out pops her kid sister, Susan, with her two children in tow.

"Well, hello," Molly says. "To what do I owe this pleasure?"

"Could you watch the kids for a couple days?"

"A couple days?" Molly says, a little taken aback. Even for Susan, who has a habit of arriving out of the blue and asking for favors, this is unexpected. "I suppose so. You got time to visit with your sister before you take off?"

"Just a minute," Susan says. "I'm heading to Huntington to do some Christmas shopping."

Molly and Susan step into the kitchen while the kids run into the living room and pull toys out of the box Molly keeps behind the couch for them, toys from when her own kids were still living at home.

Molly doesn't know what could be so important in Susan's life that she needs her to watch the kids for two days, but her little sister sure is dressed up. She's wearing nice blue jeans, a pair of boots Molly has never seen before, and a clean Members Only jacket, all of which look brand-new.

Molly has eight siblings, but Susan—nineteen years her junior—holds a special place in her heart. She's always had a spark that was irresistible, and it broke Molly's heart to see her running off with that drug dealer Clint, looking for an exciting life and a quick and easy way to make money. Molly took a different path. She married a stable man who could hold down a job, and she worked part-time to give them a little extra money. Their house isn't big, but it's not a trailer, and Molly works hard to keep it clean and looking nice.

She hates visiting Susan and seeing the world her niece and nephew are being brought up in.

"You cut your hair?" Molly says conversationally, pressing the button on her coffeemaker.

"You like it?" Susan gives her head a little shake and her short hair swings.

"I do. You look good. Not just the hair—everything. You look happy."

"I've been making a little extra money," Susan says, taking a seat at the table and crossing her legs in a relaxed manner.

"Doing what?" Molly says, getting mugs from the cupboard.

"Working as an informant for the FBI," Susan says proudly.

Molly's breath catches in her throat. She turns around slowly to face her sister, who has a sly grin and a twinkle in her eyes.

"Susan," Molly says, trying not to reveal her concern, "do you know what you're getting yourself into?"

Susan nods her head with confidence. "Don't worry about me, sis." She fills Molly in on the details of Cat Eyes's arrest and how she's been trying to find any other information that might help the new FBI agent, Mark Putnam.

"Oh, Susan," Molly says. "This sounds like it could be dangerous." She tells her sister she should get a gun, like the snub-nosed .38 Molly always has tucked into her purse, for safety.

"I'm not scared," Susan says. "Mark won't let anything bad happen to me."

Molly listens as Susan recounts how she spends her every free moment getting people to tell her things that might interest Mark. She seems to think that working for the FBI might help her get out of her situation, but Molly isn't so sure, not if Susan's spending her money on clothes instead of putting it in a bank account.

"Working for the FBI isn't the only new thing in my life," Susan tells her sister with a coy smile.

"What do you mean?" Molly says, fearing the worst.

"He's going to leave his wife for me," Susan says.

"The FBI agent?"

"We're in love. He's my ticket out of here."

"You're having an affair?" Molly asks.

"We screw like rabbits every time we get the chance. In hotel rooms, sometimes out in the woods when the weather's nice. We used to do it in his house when Kathy was out, but they had a parrot and Mark was always afraid it might say something to give us away." She imitates a parrot and squawks, *"Oh, Susan!"*

Susan giggles, but Molly isn't amused. She takes a deep breath and sits back in her chair, stunned. What is her kid sister getting herself into?

"I know you don't like taking my advice," Molly says, "but this is one time I need you to open your ears and really listen to me."

Susan rolls her eyes as if to say, *Here's the lecture I knew was coming.*

"This all sounds like trouble to me," Molly says. "You're going to get your heart broke or get yourself killed. Or both. You hear me?"

"I hear you," Susan says, rising to her feet. "But don't worry about me, okay? I'm doing great. Better than ever."

Susan goes into the living room, kneels, hugs her

children goodbye, then struts toward the door, practically bouncing on her feet. She walks to Clint's Nova and fires up the engine just as raindrops are beginning to fall. As Susan drives away, Molly wonders if her sister is *actually* having an affair with this FBI guy. She loves her little sister, but Susan tends to exaggerate, and everyone knows you can't believe one hundred percent of what she says.

But one thing Molly is certain of: if Susan isn't having an affair with Mark Putnam, she sure wants to.

CHAPTER 12

Pikeville, Kentucky. December 1987

IN THE EARLY-MORNING light, Mark stares at his newborn son, Evan, sound asleep in his crib. The boy is tiny, his head no bigger than the palm of Mark's hand.

He's perfect.

It seems impossible that such a small and innocent infant could ever grow into a big and cruel adult. Mark deals with criminals all day long, talking to informants guilty of petty crimes so that he can bust major criminals, people who have no regard for the well-being of others, and all of them started as innocent, perfect babies. What a messed-up world this is.

As he stares at his son, Mark vows to be the father his boy deserves.

"Do you have to go in today?" Kathy whispers, coming to join him at the crib.

Mark says he does. It's three days after Christmas, and

the family just got back from spending the holidays in Connecticut. Mark has been feeling antsy about taking so much time off, even if it was for Christmas and the birth of his son.

"The courthouse will be empty," he says. "I'll be able to get caught up on all my paperwork."

He drives to town, looking out at the deserted streets. It snowed at some point recently, but now all that remains are patches here and there and mounds along the road that haven't melted yet. They look more gray than white.

It's a Monday, and although it's not technically a holiday, there are only a few people in the building. Mark works for a while without interruption, organizing information for a new case involving a chop shop hidden in the hills, a place where stolen cars are stripped for parts.

Two hours later, as he's leaning back and stretching, he hears footsteps coming down the hall. There is a gentle knock on the door, and Susan pokes her head in.

"Hello, stranger," she says, smiling.

"Hi, Susan," he says, surprised at how happy he is to see her. He's missed her. "What are you doing here?"

"Oh, I was in the neighborhood and thought I'd swing by."

She steps into the room carrying a grocery bag. "Merry Christmas," she says, setting it down on his desk.

"What's this?" he asks, peering into the bag. He

sees new Nike shoes, a pair of running shorts, and a shirt. "Is this a present?" he says, exasperated. "I can't accept this."

"I wanted to say thanks," she says. "You've been good to me, Mark. The money's been welcome, but you've also given me something to be proud of. And you're nice to me." Her voice begins to crack. "Not many men have been nice to me. I just wanted to show you that I appreciate what you've done for me."

Mark feels conflicted. He's flattered, and the truth is, he's always liked her. And he's well aware that he needs her testimony to make his case.

Without giving him another chance to refuse the gift, she rushes out the door, calling, "Happy New Year!"

Mark takes a deep breath after she leaves, staring at the shoes and clothes. He dials the phone, hoping his supervisor, Trent Cavanagh, will be working the Monday after Christmas. When Cavanagh picks up, Mark tells him his informant Susan Smith just gave him a present.

"Is this the same girl who refused the payment that first time?"

"Yes."

"No big deal," Cavanagh says. "Make a note of it and put the stuff in the safe. Just don't take it home and go running in it, for God's sake." After a pause, he adds, "You're not having any problems with her, are you?"

Mark wonders how forthcoming he should be and

decides honesty is the best policy here. "She's pretty flirty," Mark admits. "I think she's got a crush on me."

Mark doesn't mention that he's got a bit of a crush on her too.

Cavanagh sighs. "Well, maintain a professional distance. But a good informant is hard to find. Do your best to keep her happy."

"Yes, sir."

"I know you've been in that office alone for a while," Cavanagh adds, "and I'm sorry about that. But we're going to have some relief for you come January. You'll be getting a new partner."

"Really?" says Mark. He's been on his own for almost a year and had forgotten someone was supposed to be using the other desk in the office.

"This guy's a pro," Trent says. "He's a veteran agent. He's done lots of undercover work, breaking some big drug cases."

This is music to Mark's ears. Aside from what Susan told him about Cat Eyes, most of her information has been about drugs. And with the chop-shop case looming, Mark just doesn't have time to deal with that.

Maybe he can pawn Susan off on the new guy.

CHAPTER 13

January 1988

DO YOU SOLEMNLY SWEAR to tell the truth, the whole truth, and nothing but the truth, so help you God?"

Susan's hand trembles as she lays it on the Bible. "I do," she says, trying to sound more confident than she feels.

She steps up into the witness box and looks out at the courtroom. She's been in courtrooms before but always sitting in the audience, looking up at the witnesses. Now she's sitting close to the judge, practically as high up as him, and the whole courtroom looks different.

Cat Eyes looks at her from the defendant's table. He has a confident expression—he doesn't think she's actually going to tell the truth. But almost everyone else in the packed courtroom is burning holes in her with their glares. Her ex, Clint, is staring at her with a hateful, intimidating expression. Cat Eyes's girlfriend, Crystal Black, sits a few feet away, looking ready to jump the barrier and claw Susan's eyes out. Other friends and family are present, all giving her the same menacing stares. What she's about to do is absolutely unheard of—she's going to publicly rat out one of their own.

To the Feds, no less.

Susan finds Mark's eyes in the courtroom. He gives her a slight nod of encouragement. But he has a worried expression. He thinks she's going to buckle under the pressure, Susan realizes.

Don't worry, Mark. I can do this, she thinks. *For you.*

"Mrs. Smith," the commonwealth attorney says. "Please state your name and spell it for the record."

Susan does.

"Do you know a man named Paul Collins, sometimes called Cat Eyes?"

"I do," she answers.

He asks her to identify Cat Eyes in the courtroom and then goes on to question her about statements he's made regarding robbing banks. As Susan answers, he reaches into an evidence box and pulls out the sawed-off shotgun. The commonwealth attorney breaks the gun to reveal that it's unloaded. After showing the judge, the jury, and the audience that it's empty, he snaps it closed and holds it high in the air.

"And is this the shotgun that you saw Cat Eyes

holding that day when he was talking about robbing banks?"

"Yes," Susan says.

Cat Eyes's expression has changed, and now he looks wounded. *How could you do this?* those feline eyes say.

Mark's expression has changed too. He looks relieved, but more than that—he looks proud of her. It gives her the confidence to sit up a little straighter.

"How do you know this is the same shotgun?" the defense attorney asks on cross-examination.

"If it ain't," Susan says, "it's one just like it, with the barrel sawed off like that. And the handle too, giving it that pistol grip."

Cat Eyes's lawyer hesitates, not sure what to ask next. He hasn't been able to rattle her yet.

"As far as I can tell," Susan offers, "there's only one difference between that gun and the one that Cat Eyes had in my house, where my kids were just a few feet away."

The lawyer perks up, hopeful that she's going to introduce some kind of reasonable doubt into the case. "So there's a difference?" he asks.

The room seems to hold its breath.

"Yeah," she says, then delivers the sucker punch. "The gun's empty now. But the one he kept in my house, where my kids sleep and play, was loaded and could have gone off at any moment."

Murmurs of surprise come from the jury box, and

the lawyer looks chagrined. He walked right into her trap.

"No more questions, Your Honor," he says.

The judge calls for a recess, and as Susan is escorted out of the courtroom by the bailiff, Mark rises and follows them out into the hall.

"That couldn't have gone better," he says to Susan. "Good work."

He looks like he wants to hug her, but that wouldn't be appropriate, especially with people filing out into the hall.

"I want you to meet someone," Mark says, taking her by the elbow and leading her to a man leaning against the wall.

The man, who's wearing a flannel shirt and a Carhartt jacket, is probably three hundred pounds. His hair is shaggy and badly in need of a trim, and his jaw is peppered with graying stubble. Susan wonders if this is a new informant.

"This is my new partner, Glen Bell," Mark tells her.

Susan feels confused for a moment. Partner? "You're an FBI agent?" Susan says to the man.

Glen laughs. "We don't all look like Yankee frat boys," he says, smacking Mark in the arm.

Mark offers no response, but something in his expression tells Susan that he doesn't much like Glen Bell. She's certain of it. Reluctantly, Susan takes the new guy's hand, which feels like a raw hamburger patty with five bratwursts sticking out of it. When she pulls her hand away, she resists the urge to wipe it on her skirt.

"I saw you up there on the stand," he says. "Very poised. Very professional. I look forward to working with you. I think we'll make a good team."

As he says this, his eyes drift down and appraise her. She's wearing a nice pencil skirt, blouse, and matching jacket. The skirt might be a little short, but otherwise she looks like an office secretary. She'd wanted to show Mark how well she cleans up, but it's this new guy's eyes that are glued to her, lingering in particular on her chest and legs. Mark seems to notice and, to her relief, rescues her from the situation by offering to walk her to her car. As they head toward the courthouse doors, she looks over her shoulder to see that Glen is still ogling her—no doubt staring at her ass in the tight skirt.

"Glen is going to be handling a lot of the drug cases while I focus on other things," Mark says. "So if you have tips along those lines, let him know. He'll treat you right."

Susan's mood has plummeted in the past few minutes. She was on such a high, feeling so proud of herself, happy that she could help Mark, the only man who's ever treated her halfway decently. Now it sounds like Mark's shoving her off on the new guy.

"So that's it?" Susan says, her eyes starting to fill with tears. "I testified against Cat Eyes and now you're done with me?"

"It's not like that," he says. "Susan, don't be silly."

Mark explains that he's been working himself to death since he arrived in Pikeville. The FBI has more to do here than two agents can handle, much less one.

"Glen is helping with the caseload," he says. "I just want you to know that you can talk to him too. Not just me."

"Okay," she says, still not happy about the situation.

As they talk, Clint and Crystal Black and a few other people walk out of the courtroom, casting glares at Susan and Mark.

"Are you going to be okay? Is it safe for you here?" Mark asks.

Susan dismisses his concern, says she'll be staying with her sister Molly for a few days. "They'll all get over it," she says. "Nobody holds a grudge around here. Give it a few weeks—everybody'll forgive and forget."

This couldn't be further from the truth. People around here can hold grudges for generations. The infamous Hatfield-McCoy feud happened in these very hollows, with neighbors killing one another precisely because no one could forgive and forget. A hundred years have passed since then, but that kind of mentality remains.

Mark walks Susan to her sister's car, waits until she's pulled out of the parking lot, then walks back to the courthouse. When he saunters past the crowd of Cat Eyes's friends, Mark tries to ignore them. He hears them muttering something that sounds like "get what's coming," but he isn't sure if they're talking about him or Susan.

Or both of them.

PART TWO

Ten Months Later

CHAPTER 14

November 1988

KATHY'S LYING ON THE floor, alternating between doing sit-ups and scissor-kicking her legs. She's worked up a sweat and wants to quit, but there's only ten minutes left on the exercise tape playing on the VCR, and a drive to lose those last five pounds of pregnancy weight keeps her going. She jumps to her feet and mirrors the instructor on the screen, kicking her legs as high as she can. She wishes she could go out running like Mark, but she doesn't have that luxury while watching two kids all day. Little Evan is bouncing in a baby walker, and Jenny is coloring in her room.

When the phone rings, Kathy considers not answering it, but she hasn't spoken to anyone except the kids all day and she's hungry for some adult interaction. She pauses the video and reaches for the phone. It's probably Susan Smith or Glen Bell, who, like Susan, is now a regular who calls on a nearly nightly basis to confide in her. She knows it can't be Mark. The chop-shop case has consumed him for the better part of a year, and most days he's usually too busy to even let her know if he'll be home for dinner.

"Hey, Kathy," Susan says. "How are you, girl?"

"Oh, I'm okay," Kathy says. Even though she and Susan have never actually met in person, Kathy has come to think of her as a friend, maybe her closest friend in Pikeville. "You?"

"Ugh," Susan moans. "I'm so sick of Glen Bell. I know the only reason he's working with me is because he wants to get in my pants. Mark never tried that, Kathy. You should know your husband's a stand-up guy."

Glen and Mark don't get along. The two work more or less separately, and the silence in the office they share is palpable and awkward. When Glen first started, Kathy insisted Mark invite him over for dinner; Glen immediately made both of them uncomfortable by whistling and commenting on Kathy's figure.

"You sure don't look like you've had two kids," he told her.

To defuse the situation—and keep Mark from losing his cool—she'd talked to Glen about her post-pregnancy workout regimen and diet. Glen confided to her that he had a hard time keeping weight off and was embarrassed about how he looked—although the extra pounds actually came in handy doing undercover work. No one expects an FBI agent to look like him.

The dinner hadn't done much to smooth over the tension between Mark and Glen, but Kathy and Glen had struck up an unlikely friendship. Soon Glen was calling at night just like Susan. Somehow, Kathy had become the confidante of the two major figures in Mark's life. She told herself she was doing it for him, that she gets personal with these people so he can stay professional, but she realized recently that she seeks these connections because of the growing gulf she feels between herself and her husband. Kathy knew being an FBI agent's wife would be challenging, but she hadn't expected this type of loneliness. Kathy feels like she's just biding her time until they can get out of Pikeville. She can't imagine living her whole life here, which is one reason she pities Susan, who is probably stuck here forever.

"Glen might look, but he'll never touch," Kathy says now, defending Glen. "He can be inappropriate at times, but he's harmless. He's just a big teddy bear."

"Humph," Susan says. "A teddy bear that won't stop staring at my tits."

"So what else is going on with you?" Kathy asks.

"Oh, Clint smacked me around again today," Susan says. "He didn't used to hit me in front of the kids, but nothing stops him now."

Kathy isn't sure if Susan's claims that Clint hits her are true. She's learned to take a lot of what Susan says with a grain of salt. But one thing is certain: with or without domestic violence, the poor girl is in a terrible living situation.

"Susan," Kathy says, "you've got to get out of there."

After Susan testified against Cat Eyes, her relationship with her ex became more and more volatile. Kathy and Mark had both hoped that Susan would use the four thousand dollars she received for testifying as a way to get out from under Clint. But instead, she gave Clint half the money. What they didn't understand until later was that it was the only way Susan could get back into the trailer to be with her children.

Neither Mark nor Kathy had known that Clint, not Susan, was the one who got custody of the two children in their divorce. Which explained the mystery of why Susan still lived there—so she could be with her kids.

"Do you think Mark could pull some strings so I could get back custody?" Susan asks.

"Sorry," Kathy says. "It doesn't work that way."

As she talks to Susan, Mark walks in, appearing tired after a long day. He looks at her quizzically, asking without words who is on the phone.

Susan, she mouths.

"Does she need to talk to me?" he asks.

She shakes her head no, and he gives her a thumbs-up.

"I should probably get dinner on the table," Kathy tells Susan a few minutes later, but Mark is already in his running clothes and heading off. The leaves are changing color and the night is coming earlier. It will be pitch-black before Mark gets back from his run. Kathy looks out the window as her husband disappears into the distance, and as she listens to Susan drone on about her situation, Kathy feels an overwhelming sadness.

I've got to stick it out. I've got to be strong for my husband.

That night, after the kids are asleep, she brings up Susan's request about custody.

"Is there anything you can do for her?" she asks as Mark brushes his teeth. "She was really useful to you, but now her whole community has turned their backs on her. She needs the agency's help."

Mark spits a stream of toothpaste into the sink.

"I'll see what I can do," he says, wiping his mouth with a towel. "But don't hold your breath that it will make much difference."

"Don't be cynical," Kathy says. "Just help her, Mark. Give her another chance."

CHAPTER 15

A WEEK LATER, MARK lies awake in bed staring at the ceiling, which in the gray light looks like the surface of the moon. Mark feels like he's floating in outer space with no way to find mooring.

He has an early meeting at the U.S. Attorney's Office in Lexington, a good three-hour drive away, but he has too much on his mind to sleep. The monumental chop-shop case devours most of his time and energy. He is making progress, and arrests are inevitable, but he hadn't realized just how much time it would take.

Having a partner he doesn't like makes matters even more challenging. Glen Bell is a loose cannon who plays by his own rules. After he'd been on the job for a month, one of the other agents in the Lexington office confided to Mark that the reason Glen had been sent to Pikeville was that no one in Lexington wanted to deal with him. So here was Mark, a rookie figuring things out as he went, paired with a rogue agent whom the higher-ups in the FBI wanted to forget about. Glen resents Mark's gung-ho attitude and hates how every supervisor in the region sees Mark as a golden boy with a bright future. Unsurprisingly, they don't make a particularly effective team.

Mark had hoped to hand Susan off to Glen as an informant. It's a smart idea in theory—Glen works mostly on drug cases, which Mark isn't particularly interested in and which Susan has a lot of information on—but Susan hates working with Glen. Mark's sympathetic; he's seen the way his partner looks at her and has heard the inappropriate comments Glen makes. Susan prefers dealing with Mark, so more often than not, he ends up being the liaison between them.

In truth, her usefulness to the agency seems to have run its course, yet Susan has come to love working for the FBI. It's given her a sense of purpose. He hates to think what would become of her if the FBI cut her loose entirely. And for better or worse, she's more Glen's informant than his now, so Mark can't close her file. Honestly, even if he could, he isn't sure he would. He's known Susan almost a year and a half, and they've grown close. When they talk, alone in the car on a backcountry road, they have great conversations, laughing and sharing stories.

He doesn't talk that way with Kathy anymore.

That is another problem weighing on him. To say his

marriage is strained is putting it mildly. But he doesn't know how to fix that relationship *and* do his job to the best of his ability.

He listens to Kathy breathing next to him in bed. He wants to roll over and put his arms around her, snuggle like they used to. When they first started dating, they'd been so intimate. Now they hardly touch, usually just a peck on the lips when he says good morning and another when he says good night. As Mark considers taking his wife into his arms, the telephone rings, shattering the silence of the house. He jumps out of bed, trying to reach it before the ringing wakes the kids.

"Putnam residence," he says, keeping his voice low. Mark hears a woman crying. He can tell at once that it's Susan.

"Can you pick me up?" she says, sobbing. "I don't have anyone else to turn to."

Helping Susan beats lying in bed tangled up in his own stressful thoughts and pining for the woman next to him, who might as well be on the other side of the Grand Canyon.

Besides, he has a fat envelope of cash he needs to deliver to Susan. Why not do it now?

"Tell me where you are," he says, "and I'll head right over."

CHAPTER 16

SUSAN STANDS IN THE shadows of the trees in her usual spot. A bank of fog hangs over the hills, glowing in the moonlight. Skeletal branches reach out of the mist like phantoms.

The night has a positively eerie feel to it, but Susan's spirits aren't dampened. As soon as Mark said he was coming, she felt better. Her life is in complete disarray. She can't get her kids away from Clint, and she can't live with him anymore. That arrangement has collapsed. All her friends in the area have stopped speaking to her, so she's not much use as an informant, which means she has no source of income except her welfare checks. She feels like the walls are closing in on her, and there's no escape hatch and no one to rescue her.

Except Mark.

When she's with him, she forgets her troubles. She's tried to put her attraction to him out of her mind, but being treated with dignity and respect—being treated like a person—is as addictive as any pill she's ever popped or line she's ever snorted.

Headlights appear through the fog, and a minute later Mark's car appears, the engine chugging exhaust into the cold night air. She climbs in. Without hesitation, Mark heads to one of their usual parking spots.

"Thanks," she says. "I just... I just can't stay with Clint anymore."

"I couldn't sleep anyway," he says.

She studies him as he drives. She usually sees him in a tie, but tonight he's dressed casually in sweats. His face glows in the light of the dashboard display. He's still as handsome as always, but he looks tired. His forehead is creased with strain, his shoulders are hunched, and his hands are strangling the steering wheel.

"I've got something for you," he says once he puts the car in park. He tugs a thick envelope from the pocket of his sweatpants and holds it out to her.

"What's that for?" she says.

"For all the work you've done for us," he says. "I talked it over with Glen and we decided that you deserved it for all the tips you've delivered."

Susan eyes him suspiciously. She can't stand Glen. If only Mark had a *little* bit of Glen's unscrupulousness—or if Glen had *a lot* of Mark's good looks...

And good manners.

And decency.

And...well, the list goes on and on.

"It's another four thousand," Mark tells her. "Hopefully you can use it to improve your situation. Maybe hire a lawyer to work out your custody issues with Clint."

Instead of snatching the envelope, Susan throws her arms around him in a tight hug. He holds her for a moment, but Susan doesn't want to let go.

It feels so good to be in his arms.

She imagines an alternate universe where the two of them met under different circumstances. She closes her eyes and pictures what that might look like.

As Mark pulls away, Susan says, "You seem stressed out. Your whole body is tense. I can feel it."

Mark lets out a deep breath, and, dropping his guard—a rarity for him—he says, "Sometimes I feel like I'm in way over my head in this job."

His vulnerability breaks her heart.

"Lean forward a little," she instructs him, and she shifts in her seat so she's on her knees. With her head near the ceiling, she reaches out to his shoulders and begins to work the muscles with her fingers. "What you need is a good massage."

She expects him to resist, to tell her this isn't appropriate. Instead, he groans with relief. She digs her fingers into his hard muscles, first on his back close to his neck, then on his upper arms around his shoulders. She rubs his neck and then runs her fingernails through his hair. He leans back against the headrest, eyes closed, and she shifts her position and kneads the muscles in his chest.

Mark opens his eyes and the two stare at each other in the half-light. He looks at her in a way she's never seen before.

Is this really happening?

Mark reaches up and gently guides her face down to his. Their lips meet, and they begin to kiss slowly. She tastes his tongue and the sweat on his lips. His stubble scratches against her chin. Susan pulls back for a moment and appraises him.

They could stop. It's not too late.

But Mark's sweatpants can't hide his arousal, and Susan takes her hand and runs it up the inside of his thigh.

Then, as if a dam has broken, their movements gain speed, and they kiss and embrace in a passionate flurry, separating only long enough to tug off each other's clothes.

CHAPTER 17

MARK SHOWERS IN THE spare bathroom, and Kathy pokes her head around the curtain.

"Did you sleep at all?" she asks.

"Not much," he says, his hair lathered with soap.

"Where did you go last night?" she asks.

"Susan," he says, unable to think of a lie.

He feels like he has guilt written all over his face, but this one-word answer is enough for Kathy. She doesn't balk at him running out in the middle of the night to meet his needy informant.

"Did you give her the money so she can hire someone to work on the custody issue?" Kathy asks.

"Yeah. I meant to tell her it was your idea," he says, "but you know how Susan is. She kept talking about her situation with Clint."

"It's no big deal," Kathy says. "I don't need credit. I hope it helps her."

She closes the shower curtain, and Mark lets the hot water spray his hair and run down his face.

He hates himself.

He can't believe how weak he was. He tells himself it was a small mistake, a little indiscretion. If only it was like college, when he could pick up a girl in a bar, screw her brains out, then never see her again.

He and his buddies had a motto: Love 'em and leave 'em; fuck 'em and forget 'em.

This doesn't have to be a big deal as long as he and Susan don't make it one, he decides. But it will not happen again, he vows.

It was just a one-night stand that didn't mean anything.

But all through his drive to Lexington and back, he keeps thinking of Susan's body pressed against his, their mouths locked in a passionate kiss. All day he feels as horny as a teenager falling in love for the first time.

That evening, when he gets back to the Pikeville office, Mark can't help himself. He calls Molly's house, where he dropped Susan off after they made love in the car.

"I was hoping you'd call," Susan says.

"I want to see you," he says. "I can't stop thinking about you."

CHAPTER 18

KATHY HANGS ORNAMENTS ON the tree in the living room while carols play on the radio. She'd put off trimming the Christmas tree, hoping it was something they could do as a family. But Mark never seems to be home these days, and Kathy decided not to wait any longer.

Putting up the tree was no small feat for her to handle solo. She'd had to drag the tree she got from the Christmas-tree lot to the house, adjust the base so the tree would stand up straight, and hang the lights, all while contending with two small children. Little Evan crawls through the room trying to put ornaments in his mouth. Jenny wants to help, but she lacks the motor skills to hook the ornaments onto the branches by herself.

Kathy stands on a chair and attaches the star to the top, then gets down and moves a few steps away to appraise the lopsided tree. She feels incredibly sad. Before she knows it, she's fighting back tears.

She doesn't know how long she can keep doing this—taking care of the children without help, never seeing her husband, never knowing when he'll be home.

She knows that after the first of the year, the FBI is finally going to start making arrests in the chop-shop case. She's hoping that Mark might have more time after that—or at least be less stressed—but even if he does, that will change when the court case gears up. He'll have to make sure his informants will testify, drive to more meetings with the U.S. Attorney. Things might not ease up until the culprits are actually in jail. But then there will be another case, and another.

Maybe things will never ease up, not as long as they're in Pikeville.

At what point will the FBI let us leave this godforsaken hellhole?

After the tree is finished and the kids are in bed, Kathy heads to the kitchen and pours herself a glass of wine. Leaving the bottle uncorked, she takes a large swallow from her glass and then refills it.

The phone rings.

She doesn't want to answer it. She figures it's probably Susan, and she's just not in the mood to hear the woman's sob stories. Glen Bell is getting on her nerves lately too.

But it might be Mark. "Putnam residence," Kathy says, trying not to sound upset.

"Where's that FBI husband of yours?" a rough male voice says.

"He's unavailable," Kathy says. "May I take a message?"

"Yeah, y'all can give him a message from us," the voice says.

Us? Kathy thinks. *Who is* us?

"Tell him we've been watching him," the man says, his voice gravelly and sinister. "We know what he does. We know where he lives. We know he leaves his pretty wife home all alone with the kids."

A cold chill shoots up Kathy's spine.

"It would be a shame if something happened to the things he loves the most," the voice says. "Lots of hiding places out in these hills. It would be easy for a person to disappear."

Kathy hangs up, unable to listen to any more. Her lungs are heaving, her heart hammering in her chest. Kathy rushes to the bedroom and throws open the closet door. Her fingers wrap around the grip of the .357 that Mark keeps hidden on the top shelf.

With trembling hands, she checks to make sure the gun is loaded. Then she hurries through the house, checking every window and door to make sure they're locked. She pulls the blinds down and switches off all the lights.

She dials Mark's office number, hoping he's there

taking care of paperwork. In truth, there's no telling where he is; he could be anywhere in the whole tri-corner area.

"Damn it!" she exclaims when there's no answer.

Kathy forces herself to sit at the kitchen table instead of pacing the house. This is where Mark finds her three hours later, the bottle of wine now empty, her hand still gripping the gun.

"Jesus, honey," he says, taking the gun from her. "What the hell is going on?"

When she tells him about the call, he's sympathetic but doesn't seem to take it as seriously as she wants him to. He doesn't feel she and the kids are in any real danger. Whoever called just wanted to intimidate him into not moving forward with the indictments for the chop-shop case. "They're just trying to scare you," he says.

"Well, it fucking worked!" she snaps.

"So don't answer the phone anymore," he says dismissively.

"I don't think that's the solution," she tells him. "What we need to do is get the hell out of Pikeville."

"How much have you had to drink?" Mark asks.

"Don't patronize me," Kathy says.

"Christ, Kathy. I don't need this shit right now."

He starts to walk out of the room, but Kathy says, "Go ahead. Walk away. Run away from our problems."

He whirls around, his eyes filled with anger. "What the

fuck do you want from me, Kathy?" he says, practically shouting. "Can't you see I'm under enough stress?"

"And I'm not? You think watching the kids all day with no help from you—*none at all*—is easy? You're gone now more than ever. I feel like a single mother. Don't you miss us? Don't you want to spend time with your children?"

These questions seem to take some of the fire out of him. *At least he feels guilty for being away from us so much,* Kathy thinks.

"I work this hard for us," he says, his voice lower but still defensive. "To make a better life for *us.*"

"Bullshit," Kathy says. "If you wanted to do what was best for us, you'd find a way to be around more. You're not gone because you have to be. You're gone so much because you don't want to be here *with your family.*"

"Oh, go to hell," Mark says, and Kathy is shocked at the bluntness of his words. "Go pass out and talk to me when you're sober."

Kathy can't take it anymore. She collapses into a chair, puts her head in her hands, and bursts into tears. Mark sits down next to her.

"I didn't mean to hurt your feelings," he says. "I just have a lot on my mind."

Kathy says nothing, just keeps sobbing. *Is that an apology?* she thinks. *Or an excuse?*

Mark takes a deep breath. "This chop-shop case will be a big feather in my cap. Between that and the Cat

Eyes arrest, I'll be able to write my own ticket. We could go anywhere." He fixes her with his stare and says earnestly, "I need you to hold on a little longer. Can you do that for me, Kathy?"

We're both struggling in different ways, she thinks, willing herself to calm down. *This is no time to be selfish. I need to support him through this.* She gives him a nod.

When Mark rises, Kathy wraps her arms around him and sobs into his chest. "I was so scared," she says.

"We're in this together," he says, rubbing her back. "We're a team."

It doesn't feel that way anymore, Kathy thinks.

The phone rings. They look at each other.

"I'll get it," Mark says.

"No," Kathy says. "I need to be strong enough to answer the phone." She reaches for the receiver. "But if it's the same person, I'm handing the phone to you," she adds. "Putnam residence," Kathy says, putting on her most no-nonsense voice. "It's the middle of the night. What do you want?"

It's a man's voice, but a different man than whoever called before. "I want to know if you're okay with your husband sticking it to my girl?" he says.

"What?"

"You know Mark is fucking Susan, right?"

In the background, Kathy hears Susan's voice shouting, "He's lying, Kathy! It ain't true!"

"Clint?" Kathy says.

"Are you going to fix this or am I going to have to do it?" Clint says.

Mark snatches the phone out of Kathy's hand. "Clint, let's just talk about this like reasonable people."

But Clint has already hung up.

CHAPTER 19

MARK IS BURNING WITH anger as he pulls up in front of Molly Davidson's house. Susan is waiting for him on the porch, wrapped in her winter coat. She smiles like a high-school girl being picked up by her prom date and practically skips over to the car. She doesn't come around to the passenger side but motions for him to roll down his window. The cold invades the warm interior of the car.

"Come inside," Susan says, her breath white in the winter air. "My sister and her husband are gone for the weekend."

"I need to talk to you," Mark says, glaring at her. "But not here."

Susan tries to coax him into the house. "Wouldn't it be nice to make love in a bed for a change?"

"Susan," Mark says, his voice almost a growl. "Get in the fucking car."

"Fine," she says and circles around to the passenger door.

As he drives away, she keeps talking about how nice it would be to spend the day inside. They could make love—maybe try some new positions—and have time for things like talking. Snuggling. Things normal couples do.

Mark doesn't say a word, and finally she gets the message. She goes quiet and waits for him to find a spot to park. Finally, he pulls down an old gravel road where they're surrounded by nothing but skeletal trees and hillsides spotted with patches of snow. A white-tail buck walks through the frozen leaves about fifty feet from the car, eyeing them suspiciously.

"Why did you tell your ex-husband about us?" Mark demands.

"Oh, that," Susan says, watching as the deer decides it's time to bound away through the woods. "He was trying to get in my pants when I came over to see the kids. I had to tell him I had a boyfriend. Otherwise, he would expect me to give in. He kept pressing me, asking who it was. I told him it was you just to piss him off. He didn't believe me. Don't worry about it."

"He called Kathy and told her I was sticking it to his girl," Mark says, unable to hide his disgust with her. "What the fuck were you thinking? Are you trying to ruin my life?"

"What did Kathy say?" Susan asks, not sounding concerned.

Mark had been able to convince his wife that Clint didn't know what he was talking about. She already knew that Susan liked to run her mouth, make up stories. Kathy had been so exhausted from their earlier fight, she'd finally shrugged it off.

"She believed me," Mark says. "But now she might start getting suspicious."

"You worry too much," Susan says. "Everything's fine."

"You can't go around telling people stuff, especially not that you and I are screwing around."

"Okay. I won't tell anyone else."

"Who else have you told?" Mark asks.

"No one, I swear."

"You promised you'd be honest with me. Remember?"

"Okay, fine," she says, and she explains that other than Clint, she hasn't told anyone about their affair since it began—but she did tell her sister Molly and some friends that she and Mark were lovers *before* they actually started sleeping together.

"You know me," she says. "I wanted it to happen but I didn't actually think you and me were going to get together."

"Jesus," Mark says, running his hand through his hair and looking out at the empty forest. "This is serious. I could lose my job."

"No one believed me," Susan says. "No one ever believes me."

Mark is furious with Susan—how could she be so

stupid? But he's also mad at himself. He *knew* Susan couldn't keep a secret. "This has to end," he says without looking at her.

"What?"

"This," he says, frustrated, pointing back and forth between them. "Us. You and me. *This* has to end."

"Fine," she says, feigning indifference. "We're just having some fun, Mark. If you don't want to do it anymore, I don't care."

He knows she's just telling him what he wants to hear.

"Take me back to my sister's house," she says. "I've got better things to do than sneak around in the woods with you."

Mark puts the car in gear, hesitates with his foot on the brake, then shifts back into park. He turns the engine off.

This is how a drug addict must feel, he thinks. *I know I shouldn't, but I just can't stop myself.*

"Not yet," he says, and he lunges toward her and plants a hard kiss on her mouth while reaching to unbuckle his belt.

CHAPTER 20

THIRTY MINUTES LATER, MARK drops Susan off in front of Molly's house without a word. She sits on the porch swing and watches him drive away, remembering how hopeful she'd been earlier as she thought about the possibility of actually making love to Mark in a bed for once, taking the time to touch and talk and just be *together*. She juxtaposes that image with what actually happened—frantic thrusts in a cramped car seat followed by instructions to hurry up and put her pants back on so they could go.

Usually when she's with Mark, she feels special.

Not today.

Today she feels the opposite.

Disposable.

She rises from the porch swing, walks inside, and collapses on the couch. She strips off her coat and leaves it lying on the floor. With Molly and her husband gone for the weekend, the house feels hauntingly empty.

Susan could say the same for her life right now—it feels empty.

She picks up the telephone and dials.

"Hello," her six-year-old daughter, Samantha, says. "Smith residence."

"Hi, honey," Susan says, her voice cracking. "It's Mommy. I just wanted to hear your voice and tell you I miss you."

CHAPTER 21

March 1989

KNOCK-KNOCK," KATHY SAYS, poking her head into the FBI office. She has little Evan on one hip and is holding Jenny's mitten-covered hand. Slung over her shoulder is a tote bag full of sandwiches and sodas. She thought she'd surprise Mark with lunch. She even brought a blanket, thinking they could spread it out on the office floor and have an impromptu indoor picnic.

But her heart sinks when she sees that Glen Bell is in the office alone.

"Hey, good-looking," Glen says. "You just missed the golden boy."

Kathy ignores the comments, as always, and asks, "Do you know where he went?"

"He didn't say," Glen says. "He's probably meeting with Susan. Those two have been thick as thieves. I thought she was supposed to be my informant now, but I guess not."

She can tell he's annoyed but doesn't want to get into it with him. In truth, she's growing tired of all the people in Mark's life who confide in her, Susan included.

Glen asks how the family is doing and tries to get shy Jenny to open up by asking which show she likes better, *Sesame Street* or *Fraggle Rock*. Kathy wants to extract herself and the kids from the situation, but Glen keeps firing questions at her. She lingers, thinking maybe Mark will show up after all. Maybe, wherever he is, it was just a quick meetup.

Glen shifts the conversation and mentions the chop-shop case, which has finally led to a dozen arrests.

"I still don't feel safe," Kathy says. "Half of them have posted bail."

Glen gives her a quizzical look. "Why don't you feel safe?"

She replies, "Mark didn't tell you? I've been getting calls at the house. Threats against me and the kids."

A sour expression comes over Glen's face. "Mark didn't mention that," he says. "He shouldn't be keeping it a secret."

He presses her for more information. Since the initial call, she's received several more. And one morning last week, right before the arrests, Mark walked out of the house to find all four of his tires slashed. He downplayed it, saying that for all they knew, it could have been kids playing a prank.

But Glen seems concerned.

"And you feel in danger?" he asks.

Kathy answers honestly. "I do. Mark doesn't seem to be taking it seriously, but I'm scared. I've been keeping our gun next to my nightstand when Mark is away. I just about shot the cable guy the other day when he came poking around our house without a uniform."

Glen tells her that if an agent's family is receiving threats, the FBI will transfer them to a different post. The agency doesn't mess around when families are at risk. "All you have to do is let the higher-ups know and you'll be out of here in no time."

"Really?"

"Yes," he says emphatically. "Your husband is well aware of this. I don't know why he wants to stick around this shithole anyway when he knows you're so unhappy here."

Kathy gets that Glen would love to get rid of Mark and have the office—and Susan—to himself for a while. But she can't help but feel angry with Mark for not explaining this to her. If anything, he made it sound like the opposite was true—that the FBI was in no hurry to transfer him and that they might be stuck in Pikeville for a while.

She realizes it's not the FBI that's holding up their transfer away from Pikeville.

It's Mark.

She's going to have to take matters into her own hands and make him understand that they need to leave.

"Anyway," Glen says, "I'll tell him you stopped by."

"Oh, he'll know I came by," she says. "Mark and I are going to have a serious conversation when he gets home tonight."

CHAPTER 22

April 1989

SUSAN IS DRUNK.

And miserable.

She sits on a bar stool in a hole-in-the-wall road-house out in the boondocks. The air is thick with cigarette smoke, the jukebox is playing Merle Haggard, and the walls are adorned with posters of scantily clad women in suggestive poses holding beer bottles.

Two men tried to hit on Susan when she first arrived, but she told them to stick their beers where the sun didn't shine, and she's been left alone since then.

Mark has gone to Florida to start a new life with his family, and Susan is heartsick over it. She knows it was stupid to fall for the guy, but she couldn't help herself. She'd never had a man take such an interest in her.

Never had a man make her feel she mattered.

"Another," she tells the bartender, her words slurred, her vision blurred.

"You sure?" he asks. "How you getting home, little lady?"

Susan glares at the mountain of a man with a neck like a Christmas ham. "I work for the FBI," she sneers. "If you don't want a dozen agents coming down here and seeing what goes on in your back rooms, you'll pour me as many damn beers as I want."

He shakes his head, more irritated than scared by her threat, and gives her another draft. "Last one," he says. "On the house."

She yanks the beer toward her, sloshing the liquid on the bar top, and takes a big sip.

What hurts the most is that he didn't even say goodbye.

After their argument about her mentioning the affair to Clint, they'd gotten together only a few more times. The sex had been quick and loveless. In the beginning, their rendezvous had felt romantic. But by the end, Mark seemed angry with her and was clearly just using her to get off, quickly and dispassionately.

Susan kept her distance, not wanting to seem desperate or scare him away. She badly wanted him to realize on his own how important she was. But earlier today, after almost a month of silence, she'd finally given in and visited his office. She'd had a good cover story too—she wanted to talk to him about a dirty cop she'd known in Chicago when she lived there with Clint. She was going to propose that she and Mark take a trip up there to see the guy. Mark's supervisors would love it if he busted a dirty cop. Plus, it would be a chance for the two of them to get away, have some one-on-one time, make love in a hotel room for once.

Maybe she and Mark could reconnect.

But when she walked into the office, she could see Mark was gone; his desk was empty of the file folders and family pictures that used to be there. Glen Bell, happy as a pig in mud to see her, told her that Mark and his family had moved to Florida.

Susan had rushed out of the courthouse and headed straight to the closest bar.

She knew getting involved with a married man was a bad idea. She knew it wouldn't last forever. But she'd never thought he'd leave her without even saying a proper goodbye.

Despite the logical part of her brain telling her that he'd used her, that she didn't mean half as much to him as he did to her, she finds herself wishing she'd told him that she loved him. Even if he didn't say it back— even *when* he didn't say it back—at least he would know how she felt.

Susan finishes her beer and rises from the bar stool. She doesn't know what time it is or where she's sleeping tonight. She can't stand the I-told-you-so looks she knows she'll get from her sister Molly right now, and Clint's place is no longer an option. Susan filed a restraining order against him last week, and he retaliated by telling the welfare offices in Kentucky and West Virginia that she's been double-dipping. The final few hundred-dollar bills from her last FBI payment are all that she has to live on unless she can convince Glen Bell to go for the idea about the dirty cop she was going to pitch to Mark.

As she staggers across the concrete floor, she pictures Glen Bell trying to kiss her, and suddenly the contents of her stomach feel like acid burning to get out. She runs into the parking lot, collapses to her knees in the gravel, and retches up hot foamy beer.

When her stomach is finally empty, she stays on her knees, eyes closed, breathing in the fresh air.

"Well, look what the cat dragged in," she hears a familiar female voice say.

Susan squints into the glare of the building lights, seeing the blurry shapes of a group of people.

One is Clint.

Another, walking toward her, is Crystal Black.

Susan rises to her feet, wiping vomit off her lips with her sleeve.

"I hear your boyfriend moved to Florida," Crystal says snidely.

"I hear yours moved to prison," Susan quips.

"You bitch!" Crystal snaps, pushing Susan with both hands.

Susan feels weightless for a moment, then her back collides with the gravel, and Crystal is on top of her.

Susan tries to fight back, but she's too wasted. Crystal rains blows down on her.

"Clint," Susan pleads, looking around for the father of her children, "help me."

"Sorry," he says insincerely. "I got a restraining order that says I can't get near you."

Susan curls into a ball and uses her hands to protect her head from the worst of the punches. Crystal lands a few more blows against her ribs and her stomach, then straightens up, huffing. "You've seen too many movies," Crystal says, standing over Susan. "You think you can just rat out your people and get away with it? Life don't work like that around here. Quit helping the FBI or you're going to get yourself killed."

Crystal and the others walk away, leaving Susan lying on the ground. She spits a glob of bloody saliva into the gravel and rolls over onto her back. She decides it's not worth getting up.

She's just going to close her eyes and fall asleep right here.

CHAPTER 23

SUSAN WAKES UP TO bright artificial light.

She blinks and looks around, trying to figure out where she is. She's in a hospital room, that much is obvious, but she can't remember how she got here. She tries to sit up, and her ribs ache with pain. The memory of Crystal Black attacking her in the parking lot floods her brain.

She wants to break down and cry, but she's too tired to even do that.

If this isn't rock bottom, she thinks, *I don't know how much more I can take. I don't know how I can keep falling.*

Her mouth feels as dry as cotton, and she looks around for something to drink. With perfect timing, a nurse walks in with a tray of food.

"How are you feeling?" the nurse says with a smile.

"Like I had too much to drink and someone beat the shit out of me," Susan says.

"Sounds about right," the woman says, offering her a cup with a straw sticking out. "I've got the business card of a state trooper if you want to file charges."

What good will it do? Susan thinks. "No, thanks." She sits up and takes a drink of water. "Anything broken?" she asks.

"Nope," the nurse assures her. "You'll have some aches and pains for about a week, but there's no permanent damage. You'll be fine and so will the baby."

Susan stares at her. "Excuse me?"

The nurse looks sympathetic. "Did you not know about the pregnancy? I hope it's good news."

Susan collapses back onto the bed, unsure how to feel.

"I'll have the doctor check on you in a few minutes," the nurse tells her. "Is there anything I can get for you?"

Susan faces her. "Can you give me some documentation confirming I'm pregnant?"

When she's alone, Susan breaks down and cries. After a few minutes, she wipes away her tears and places one hand on her abdomen.

"It's okay," she says. "Daddy's going to do right by us. Don't you worry."

CHAPTER 24

Miami, Florida. May 1989

MARK CAN SEE PALM TREES from his window at the FBI's Miami office. Sunlight pours in, a sharp contrast to the gray skies he just left behind.

He can't believe how fast the transfer occurred. The Bureau had everything lined up in two weeks. There was a flurry of packing, and before he knew it, a moving truck was parked in front of his house.

Everything about his new life in Florida is different. For most of the time he'd been in Pikeville, he'd worked in a tiny office by himself; here, he's in a huge office with more than thirty agents. Before, he covered an expansive rural area with hollows hidden in the woods, abandoned coal roads snaking through the hills, and dozens of small communities with populations in the hundreds or even dozens. Now he's working in a major urban area with a dense population, diverse demographics, and completely different crimes.

Home life is different too.

Kathy is smiling again.

They took the kids to the beach over the weekend and everyone had a ball building sandcastles and getting knocked over by waves. Kathy looked like she'd shaken off her depression overnight.

Mark is glad to be in Florida if for no other reason than the temptation of Susan Smith isn't available to him. It's just a matter of time, he hopes, before the whole thing becomes an unpleasant but distant memory.

The phone ringing on Mark's desk jolts him out of his thoughts.

"Hey, buddy, how's the Sunshine State treating you?"

"Hi, Glen," Mark says, trying to sound at least somewhat glad to hear from his old partner.

Glen says he's calling to see when Mark will be back in Pikeville. He has to return in order to wrap up work on various investigations, principally the chop-shop case. Mark says he's scheduled to be there next week.

"I need your help when you're here," Glen says. "Dealing with Susan."

Mark groans. The last thing he wants to do is deal with Susan.

"She's absolutely gone off the deep end," Glen says. "She's got some crazy scheme in mind about catching a dirty cop in Illinois that might actually work if she can get her shit together long enough to make it work. She has no money, can't see her kids. She's calling me nonstop for help, asking about you, wanting to talk to you. She's been spreading some pretty wild rumors up here."

Mark closes his eyes and squeezes the bridge of his nose. "You know you can't believe half of what comes out of Susan's mouth," Mark says, practically parroting what Trooper Neil Whittaker once told him— although, in reality, Mark had found that Susan was always honest with him.

"I know, I know," Glen says. "I'm just telling you you'll need to talk to her when you're in town. Try to rein her in some. I know she was a big help to you. I want to work with her."

I'll bet you do, Mark thinks. "I'll talk to her," he says. "Just don't give her my phone number down here, all right?"

"Oh," Glen says, "was I not supposed to do that?"

Mark's heart sinks. For the rest of the day, his stomach clenches whenever his phone rings. When he finally heads home, he feels like he's dodged a bullet. But when he walks into the townhome they're renting, he spots a familiar sight: Kathy on the telephone.

"It's Susan," Kathy says, handing the phone to him. "She wants to talk to you."

CHAPTER 25

Eastern Kentucky. June 1989

WHEN MARK AND HIS family left Pikeville, the spring bloom had only just begun, and most of the trees had still been bare. But now, as he steers the Ford Tempo he rented at the airport in Huntington through the winding roads, the hills look beautiful, lush and green.

Mark hadn't realized how much he'd wanted to get out of Kentucky until they'd left. Now that he's back, he feels like he's returned to a bad dream.

It feels like he'll never be able to truly escape.

Mark couldn't sleep last night, knowing he would have to confront Susan when he got here. Ever since her phone call, he's been wondering if her claim of being pregnant is true or another of her wild stories.

He plans to go straight to the FBI office and get a few hours' worth of work done before heading to the hotel room Glen's booked for him. Mark and Kathy haven't sold their house yet—doing some repairs on it is one of the things Mark needs to take care of while he's in town—but there's no furniture in it anymore, so he can't stay there.

"Hey, buddy," Glen says when Mark walks in. "Welcome back."

Glen's cheerfulness at seeing him is completely insincere. They'd barely tolerated each other when they worked together; they'd certainly never been buddies. Frankly, Mark had been hoping Glen wouldn't even be in the office when he arrived, but no such luck.

"Susan was here earlier," Glen tells him. "She left something for you on your desk."

Mark picks up the slip of paper: a medical report confirming her pregnancy. Mark studies the paper, aware that Glen is staring at him, watching to see his reaction. He's certain Glen looked at it. In fact, he'd put money on Susan having told Glen that the baby is Mark's.

Mark puts the paper down, feigning indifference, and opens his briefcase. "Do you have transcripts from the chop-shop hearings?" Mark asks, acting as if the document hasn't fazed him.

"Sure," Glen says, clearly disappointed that Mark doesn't want to talk about Susan's news.

A few hours later, Mark packs up his briefcase and heads to the car. Glen booked him a room at the Landmark Hotel, one of the few decent places in town, and he makes the short drive there.

Once in his room, Mark pulls off his tie, loosens his collar, takes his pistol off his belt, and hides it in the bedside drawer next to the Bible. He kicks his shoes off and lies back on the bed. He had wanted to go for a run, and he still needs to eat dinner, but he feels dog-tired and considers just going to sleep.

Before he can do anything, though, there's a knock on his door. "I know you're in there," Susan calls.

When Mark opens the door, she stalks in, then turns on her heel and faces him. She is wearing cutoff shorts and a V-neck shirt that exposes the gold cross she always wears. She looks fatigued herself, her eyes watery, maybe from drinking, maybe from drugs.

"Let me guess," he says. "Glen Bell told you where I was staying."

"He booked me a room here too," Susan says. "He wanted to make sure you didn't ignore me."

That interfering asshole. Mark can just picture Glen laughing to himself as he set the trap.

"Look, I just got into town," Mark says, exasperated. "I was planning to call you. I'll be here for several days. There's plenty of time for us to talk."

"Okay," Susan says, plopping down on Mark's bed. "Let's talk."

The medical report noted she was due in November, which means she's almost halfway along now, but she doesn't look pregnant to Mark. Then again, he can't remember how a pregnant woman should look at this point. *Of course I don't remember,* he thinks. *I wasn't around much when Kathy was pregnant. I was always working.*

"What are you going to do about our baby?" Susan demands.

"Are you sure it's mine?" he asks, then immediately regrets the question.

She looks deeply hurt. "I know I don't mean anything to you," Susan says, fighting back tears. "But I care about you. I wasn't screwing around with other people. This baby," Susan adds, pointing to her abdomen, "is yours."

"Well, why weren't you on birth control?" Mark says. "Jesus, Susan, how could you be so stupid?"

"If you're so goddamn smart, why didn't you wear a condom?" Susan says. "Didn't they teach you in the FBI Academy to wear rubbers when you fucked your informants?"

"Go to hell," Mark growls.

They glare at each other for a few seconds, both shocked that their argument has risen to this level of hostility.

Finally, calmly, Susan says, "We need to stop fighting. We're having a baby. What are we going to do?"

Hesitantly, Mark says, "I think you should have an abortion."

Susan stomps over to him and slaps him across the face. "I'm not having an abortion!" she shouts. "This is *our* baby. *Ours.* You think about that!"

She storms out of the room, slamming the door behind her.

Mark, his cheek stinging from the slap, paces around the room, his fists clenched. He kicks over a chair. He takes his suitcase and hurls it against the wall, spilling all the contents out. He leans over the bed and begins punching a pillow. He wants to roar but bites back his rage because he doesn't want anyone in the hotel to hear him.

Finally, he falls back onto the bed, his hands clutching his hair, wondering how he can get out of the mess he's gotten himself into.

CHAPTER 26

SUSAN DIDN'T RETURN THAT night, but as Mark is getting dressed the next morning, she knocks on his door. As soon as he opens it, she barges in and stomps over to his suitcase.

She pulls out a pair of his shorts and a T-shirt. "I gotta borrow these," she says. "I barely fit in my old clothes anymore, and I didn't bring enough clothes when I checked into the hotel."

She also says she needs to use his phone to call her sister because the one in her room isn't working. He doesn't believe her, but he doesn't have time to argue. "I'm sorry, but I have to go. I'm due at the U.S. Attorney's Office," he tells her as he finishes tying his tie and holsters his gun.

"You might not care about me," she says, "but I'm going to make sure you care about this baby."

"Just shut the door behind you when you leave," he says. "We'll talk tonight. We'll figure this out."

He drives the three hours to Lexington in a trance, but as he walks into the building, he puts up a façade of calm professionalism. On the inside, he is a nervous mess, his mind spinning with various options, none of which seem good. It is after five o'clock before he can head back to Pikeville, his stomach in knots.

He hoped to have a few minutes in his room alone before Susan came calling. But she is already there. She never left. She is sitting on his bed, wearing his shorts and T-shirt, flipping through the TV channels.

Susan's eyes are bloodshot from crying; her hair is disheveled and greasy. Her complexion, once smooth and unblemished, looks blotchy. Mark tries to remember the pretty mountain girl he met in the clearing two years ago, the one with the bright smile and sassy personality. She'd looked like a young woman with a promising future ahead of her. Now she looks like a homeless person with no hope of bettering her situation.

My God, he thinks. *I've ruined this poor girl's life.*

Then another thought occurs to him.

How am I going to stop her from ruining mine?

Susan turns the TV off and Mark puts his pistol in the bedside drawer. He tugs off his tie and sits on the bed opposite her.

"Well," she says. "Are you ready to talk?"

"Let's go for a drive," he says. "We always had the best talks when we were parked somewhere. Just the two of us. Alone."

CHAPTER 27

THE SUN IS SETTING as Mark and Susan drive out of town. He parks on an old mine road about fifteen miles from Pikeville. The two of them have been meeting in places like this off and on for two years, first in a professional capacity and then in a romantic one. They make small talk for a few minutes, circling around the inevitable conversation. The night gets darker and darker, and soon the only light is coming from the dashboard. Finally, Mark decides that he can't put it off any longer.

I've got to face this, he thinks. "When the baby's born," he tells Susan, "we'll do a paternity test to make sure it's mine."

"It's yours," she says.

He can't see her face clearly in the dim light, but he can tell by her tone that she's angry.

"If it's mine," he continues, "I'll talk to Kathy, and she and I can adopt the baby. We'll raise it as our own."

Mark sees Susan raising her arm to slap him like she did last night. This time, he's ready and catches her wrist. She thrashes against him, and he pushes her back into her seat.

"You think I'm a bad mother?" she says, practically screaming. "You think I can't raise this baby?"

"You lost custody of your own kids to a drug dealer!" Mark says, unable to hold the words back. They've been headed toward this fight for a long time, and he decides it's time to finally have it out.

"I love those kids," she says, sobbing. "It breaks my heart that I don't get to see them."

"Susan, you're a mess. I tried to help you, but no matter what chances you're given, you piss them away."

"You tried to help me?" she says. "How? By getting me pregnant and telling me to get an abortion? Some help you are."

"Susan," Mark says angrily, "what is it you want from me? What is it you think will get us out of this situation?"

Susan takes a few seconds to catch her breath. "I don't want out of this situation," she says. "I want to be with you, Mark. I want you to be there when the baby is born. I want you to put your name on the birth certificate. I want you to leave Kathy and be with me. Take me to Florida. Get me out of this hellhole so I don't ever have to come back."

As she speaks, her voice changes from aggressive to pleading.

"We can be happy together," she says. "I know we can. I love you, Mark, and I know you love me too. The passion we felt—that was real. We can be together if you'll just follow your heart. Do what you want to do instead of what you think you should do. Can't you see us together, walking on the beach, holding hands with our son or daughter?"

"I already have that with Kathy and our kids," Mark says coldly. "What you're describing is a fantasy that will never happen. You need to step out of dreamland so we can have a real discussion about what to do."

"You asshole!" Susan screams. "You ruined my life! I did nothing but help you. I launched your career. I was there for you when your wife wasn't. And you used me like a piece of meat you could just throw away!"

"You used *me!*" Mark roars back, his fury surging to the surface. "You're trying to entrap me. For all I know, you got pregnant on purpose. You planned this, didn't you?"

His words have the desired effect; she's quiet for a moment. "You're a bastard," she eventually mutters, her voice cracking.

"And you're a fucking train wreck. You shouldn't raise this baby. If it's mine, Kathy and I—"

"There is no way your whore of a wife is going to raise my baby."

"You of all people have no right to call my wife a whore."

"What's that supposed to mean? Are you saying *I'm* a whore?"

"Just leave Kathy out of this," Mark says, balling one hand into a fist.

"Or what? You'll hit me? Go ahead," Susan taunts. "Men have been hitting me my whole life. Go ahead and prove you're no better than any other man I've ever known."

"Don't think I won't."

"Your wife was arrested for prostitution," Susan says matter-of-factly. "If that doesn't make her a whore—"

Mark punches her in the jaw, sending her head into the windshield. It's a hard blow—he can't believe he just did that—but Susan only laughs and says, "That all you got? That's nothing."

"Go to hell, you bitch!"

"No," Susan spits. "I'm going to make *your* life a living hell. I'll come down to Florida if I have to. I'll tell all your FBI buddies that the way you get ahead is to sleep with your informants."

"Shut up, Susan. I'm fucking warning you!"

"I'll come to your house"—she's verbally twisting the knife now—"and put our baby in your daughter's arms and she's going to look at you and say, 'Daddy, why does Susan's baby have the same last name as us?'"

Mark's rage erupts. "Shut up, you goddamn bitch!"

He slams the palm of his hand over her mouth and shoves her head against the window. Susan bites his hand, hard, and he jerks it away. His teeth clenched, growling like an animal, Mark swings at her again. But she kicks and squirms, and his fist lands against the door, sending shooting pain through his wrist that only enrages him more.

She lunges at his face, screaming, her hands like claws, but he stops her by seizing a fistful of hair and yanking her head back, exposing her throat. He grabs her neck, first with one hand and then both. His long fingers encircle her neck and he squeezes. Her neck is small in his big hands. She digs her nails into his arms, and he tightens his grip. She kicks and thrashes, but he holds on.

She makes no sound—not a grunt or a gasp.

Her airway is blocked.

Her muscles begin to relax.

Her body sags flaccidly in his grip.

When Mark lets go of her, she flops against the passenger door.

He can't see her expression in the dark, but he assumes she's unconscious. He breathes heavily from the exertion for a few moments, then reaches over to give Susan a small shake to rouse her.

Her body remains completely limp. Trying not to panic, Mark grips her arms and drags her out of the car, her limbs loose, her head dangling unnaturally.

He gently lays her in the gravel and kneels to examine her.

Her eyes are open, catching the moonlight, but there is no life in them.

Susan is gone.

CHAPTER 28

OH, FUCK.

What now?

It's only a few hours until sunrise. Mark drives back to the hotel, though he knows there's no way he'll sleep. He strips off his clothes, which stink of sweat and panic, and takes a long hot shower. Afterward, he dresses in a daze. His arms are scratched from Susan's nails, but a long-sleeved shirt easily covers the marks.

The sky is still a dark blue when he heads back out. There is no activity in the town this early. As he walks across the parking lot, his shoes click loudly in the silence; he turns around, thinking he is being followed.

When he arrives in Lexington, the sun is bright. He parks his car at a meter in front of the U.S. Attorney's Office building, places his bubble on the dash so he won't get a ticket, and walks inside like it's any other day.

He doesn't let on that his mind is anywhere but on the job. It's actually pretty chilling to realize how easy it is to compartmentalize his brain. Even though he thinks about the situation with Susan nonstop, he's also able to function in conversations with the attorneys and make small talk with other agents.

Later that day, he drives back to Pikeville and gets a bite to eat while he waits for the sun to go down. Then he drives out of town in the gloom of twilight. He takes a turn at Harmon Branch Road, about ten miles outside of Pikeville, and then another down an old mine road. He and Susan met here often.

It is one of the places they made love.

He parks the car next to a steep ravine with mounds of rock excavated from the mine piled on the opposite side of the embankment. He takes a deep breath, climbs out of the car, and circles back to the trunk. He sticks the keys in and pops the trunk open.

Susan's dead body lies contorted inside.

He'd expected her corpse to stink after sitting in the hot trunk all day, but there isn't much smell yet. He tugs off the shorts and shirt that belong to him. Underneath, she wasn't wearing anything, so her body is now completely naked except for the small gold cross around her neck.

It's difficult to wrestle her out of the trunk, but he

finally manages it. Carrying her like a bride over a threshold, he walks to the edge of the ravine.

"Goodbye, Susan," he says, and he kisses her forehead.

Then he heaves her dead body down the embankment.

CHAPTER 29

Miami, Florida. Two Weeks Later

MARK MAKES IT TO the toilet just in time. Diarrhea exits his body like hot water out of an open tap. His forehead is clammy, and he feels feverish.

He washes his hands, splashes water on his face, and straightens his tie. He looks at himself in the mirror. He's losing weight, and the circles under his eyes grow darker each day. He can't get any sleep. He wonders how anyone can look at him and not notice that something is seriously wrong.

Out in the kitchen, Kathy has just prepared breakfast for the children. Jenny scribbles with a crayon in her *Little Mermaid* coloring book with one hand while spooning Lucky Charms into her mouth with the other. Evan eats a Pop-Tart with both hands.

Kathy starts to pour Mark a cup of coffee.

"No coffee," he says, waving her off and reaching for a bottle of Pepto-Bismol in the cupboard. "Thanks anyway." He gulps the thick liquid directly from the bottle.

"Do you still have that stomach bug?" Kathy asks. "I wish you'd see the doctor."

"No time," he says, putting the bottle of Pepto into his briefcase. "It will pass."

"You work too hard," she says.

He doesn't argue. It's true. He hasn't slowed down, because he doesn't want anyone—including Kathy—to suspect that anything is wrong. He figures the best way to hide in plain sight is to do good work.

He kisses both children goodbye and then gives Kathy a long hug. She smiles up at him. Miami has been good for her. She looks tan, healthy, and happy—a sharp contrast to how she'd been at the end of their time in Kentucky.

He drives to work with the windows open, letting the breeze fill the car and cool his clammy skin. Palm trees line the road, and the smell of salt is thick in the air.

Mark enters the FBI's Miami office and greets the secretary with his usual friendly smile.

"Good morning," she says. "Graham wants to see you. Told me to send you in straightaway."

She delivers the message with a smile, but Mark's gut seizes up. Graham Blevins is the special agent in charge of the Miami office, and if he wants to see Mark first thing, it's important.

"Come on in," Blevins says when Mark knocks. "Shut the door behind you, please."

Mark takes a seat across from him. The office is austere, the mahogany desk uncluttered, the walls adorned only with his diplomas and certificates and a photo of Blevins with President Bush.

"I'll get right to it," he says, taking a single sheet of paper and sliding it across the desk to Mark.

They know about Susan.

Mark tries to keep his hands from trembling as he lifts the piece of paper. He expects to see a subpoena to appear before the Pike County grand jury. Or an indictment. Mark wonders if he'll have to turn over his badge right now. He might be taken out of the office in handcuffs.

But then his mind registers what he's looking at. The paper isn't an indictment—it's a commendation. It's a memo from the U.S. Attorney's Office praising Mark's work on the chop-shop case.

"You've made the FBI proud," Blevins says, extending his hand as he rises.

Mark doesn't hide his smile as he shakes his boss's hand.

I can't believe it, Mark thinks when he returns to his desk and reads the commendation again. He knows that someone—the state police, the FBI, or both—will investigate Susan's disappearance eventually. It will look suspicious if he stays quiet and doesn't mention she's missing.

He picks up the phone and dials the number for Susan's sister Molly from memory.

"Molly," he says. "This is Mark Putnam. I'm trying to reach Susan. Do you know where she is?"

There's a long pause on the other end of the line.

"I haven't heard from her," she says finally. "It's not like Susan not to call."

Mark tells her that his former partner in the Pikeville office hasn't heard from her either.

"The last time she called me," Molly says, her voice uneven, "she said she'd just told you the baby was yours."

"That's ridiculous," Mark says. "You know you can't believe half of what Susan says."

"She showed me the paperwork," Molly says. "Said she left it on your desk."

"Look," he says, "let's not argue about the father of her baby. Once we know Susan's safe, I'll take a paternity test to prove she's just making up stories."

Mark tells Molly that if she doesn't hear from Susan in a few days, she should report her missing. He's surprised when Molly replies, "Why don't you just stay down there in Florida and mind your own business. You've done enough harm to Susan."

Mark opens his mouth to object, but he's too late—there's only a dial tone on the line. Flustered, he sets the phone down. He thinks hard about the next call, wondering if he's going too far, but he decides to make it anyway.

"Kentucky State Police," says a cheerful voice on the other line. "How may I direct your call?"

"This is Mark Putnam from the FBI," he says. "I'd like to report a missing person."

PART THREE

Nine Months Later

CHAPTER 30

Lexington, Kentucky. April 1990

SUPERVISORY SPECIAL AGENT Pete Pearson is sitting in his office signing off on routine reports when Agent Jack Cornell knocks on his door and asks if he can talk to him.

"Sure," Pearson says, putting his pen down as Cornell walks in. "What's up?" Pearson sits forward in his chair. He can tell his colleague has something serious on his mind. The agent has done impressive work in the Lexington office since he transferred from Pikeville three years ago.

Cornell takes a seat and says, "Listen, we may have a situation down in Pikeville."

Pete Pearson frowns. Pikeville is supervised by the Covington office of the FBI, but Pearson knows about most of what goes on in the state. He hasn't heard much out of the Pikeville office since Mark Putnam transferred away a year ago. The

hardworking rookie had made some big busts—
a bank robbery, a stolen-automobile ring—but he'd
moved on to Miami. The guy there now, Glen Bell,
is a veteran but hardly a model agent, and he
hasn't done much since Putnam left as far as Pearson
knows.

"I was down in the Pikeville area doing some interviews on one of our cases," Cornell says, "and I figured
I'd swing by the state police office and say hello to some
folks. One of the detectives—Steven Gerards, you
might know him—he told me they've been working a
missing-persons case."

"Okay," Pearson says, waiting to hear what this has
to do with the FBI.

"The missing girl used to be an informant for us,"
Cornell tells him. He goes on to explain that the state
police investigation has turned up all kinds of rumors
about the girl. "Apparently, before she disappeared, she
was telling people that she and Mark Putnam were
having an affair," Cornell says.

"Putnam's been gone since last year," Pearson says.

"So has the girl," Cornell says. "She went missing
last summer right around the time Putnam was back in
town finishing up some work on old cases. The state
police want to interview him, but according to them,
the FBI's been stonewalling them."

Pearson sits back in his seat. He's been in the FBI
twenty years, ten as a supervisor in the Lexington

office, and he's never heard of a state police agency actively investigating one of their agents.

"Mark was one of the people who reported her missing," Cornell says, "but they still think he might be involved somehow."

"We can't have these kinds of rumors flying around," Pearson says. "Let me make some calls."

As Jack Cornell leaves, Pearson calls the captain in the Pikeville state police office, Isaac Wood, a man he's worked closely with on and off over the past several years.

"I just heard a rumor that you're looking into one of our agents in a missing-persons case," Pearson says, as politely as possible.

"You know my detective Steven Gerards?" Wood asks.

"Yes," Pearson says. "He does good work." He means it too—Detective Gerards is known to be careful, methodical, and thorough. He has good instincts and he follows them until he finds answers.

"Steven's looked into this case for the better part of a year," Wood says. "We don't have any evidence, but your guy Putnam might very well be involved."

Pearson doesn't like the sound of this.

"And even if he isn't," Wood continues, "this girl was one of your informants and she's gone missing. The FBI has a responsibility to find out what happened to her."

"I agree," Pearson says.

"That's music to my ears," Wood says. "We've been hitting nothing but brick walls trying to deal with you Feds. You've got access to the one guy we need to talk to."

Pearson discusses the situation with Wood for a few minutes. The FBI doesn't have jurisdiction in local investigations, but if the woman was kidnapped and taken across state lines, it can be considered a federal case. No one has any real idea if she was kidnapped or murdered or if she just ran off, but it's the simplest way to justify the FBI's involvement.

"This needs to be a real investigation," Wood says. "This better not be some fake inquiry where all you're trying to do is cover your own asses."

"Don't worry," Pearson says. "I'll assemble a team of some of our best agents, all with experience in Kentucky, and bring them down to Pikeville."

"Whoever you put in charge, let me know, and I'll have Steven Gerards get in touch with the case files."

"I can tell you who it is right now," Pearson says. "Me. I'm going to be leading the team."

CHAPTER 31

Pikeville, Kentucky. May 1990

TWO FBI SEDANS PULL into the parking lot of the Landmark Hotel at dusk, and five agents exit. One of them, Supervisory Special Agent Pete Pearson, is carrying two pizza boxes. He leads the other agents across the parking lot as the setting sun ignites the surrounding Kentucky hills in an eerie red glow, adding an ominous weight to what the five men are about to discuss.

"Meet in my room in fifteen," Pearson says, and he climbs the stairs to the second floor.

The other agents—Jack Cornell, Tracy McGovern, Boyd Robertson, and Daryl Christopher—go to their rooms, make quick calls to their wives or children, then head to their supervisor's room for a long night of work.

They've spent the past week reviewing the Susan Daniels Smith investigation that the state police have been pursuing. As far as they can tell, the state investigator who'd been looking into Susan's disappearance left no stone unturned. It was good police work, but it's led to nothing but dead ends thus far.

Susan Smith, they've discovered, had plenty of enemies.

Her ex-husband has a history of criminal behavior, and before her disappearance, Susan filed a restraining order against him, claiming assault. She's also testified against a bank robber known as Cat Eyes, and retribution is a legitimate possibility. And she was apparently working to make connections with drug dealers out of state in an effort to help the FBI nail a dirty cop in Illinois.

The problem is, many people who were once close to Susan had turned their backs on her because of her work as an FBI informant, and they were naturally uncooperative when the agency came around asking questions. Of those who would talk, several said they assumed she'd just run off and would turn up again sooner or later.

The investigation seems to be at an impasse. The good news is the FBI is caught up on everything the state police were able to find in their nearly yearlong investigation. The bad news is they don't know where to go from here. Despite this technically being a kidnapping case, they're all working under the assumption she's likely been murdered.

But by whom?

"Okay," Pete Pearson says as the FBI agents discuss the case over pizza, "let's just go around the room." He stands facing his four agents, who are seated on the two beds. "One by one, I want to hear what you think might have happened."

He points first at Agent Jack Cornell.

"Cat Eyes probably had her killed," Cornell theorizes. "Either he ordered the hit from prison or people loyal to him took it upon themselves to avenge him. We know Crystal Black assaulted her once. Maybe she came back to finish the job."

"Okay," Pearson says, turning to Tracy McGovern. "What do you think?"

"Her ex-husband did it," McGovern states. "He has a criminal record. There's a history of domestic violence. We all know that wife-beaters often graduate to wife-killers."

Pearson turns to Boyd Robertson.

"I think it was the drug dealers out of Chicago," Robertson says. "I bet she went up there trying to make drug contacts, and something happened to her. If there really is a dirty cop involved, she was dealing with a whole new league of drug dealers than what she was used to."

Pearson nods, considering this. "Okay, what about you, Daryl? What do you think happened?"

Daryl Christopher takes a deep breath and says, "I think Mark Putnam killed her."

"You don't really mean that, do you?" says Pearson, looking around at the other agents, who all seem shocked too.

"Think about it," Christopher says. "If there's any truth to the rumors that they were having an affair, then he certainly had motive."

"If what you're suggesting turns out to be true," Pearson says, "it would be unprecedented." In the eighty-year history of the FBI, no acting agent had ever been convicted of a homicide.

"If he weren't an agent," Christopher continues, "he'd go right to the top of the suspect list, wouldn't he?"

The agents look around at one another, wondering if anyone will argue with Christopher's logic.

No one does.

"Okay," Pete Pearson says finally. "Let's zero in on Putnam. If it turns out he's clean, we'll scratch him off our list and move on. But if we find anything…"

He doesn't finish the sentence. Everyone in the room understands the weight of what they're about to do: investigate one of their own.

CHAPTER 32

Miami, Florida. May 1990

PETE PEARSON WAITS IN the conference room at the FBI's Miami office with Agent Jack Cornell and Detective Steven Gerards from the Kentucky State Police. None of the men speak. They've agreed to let Pearson take the lead in the interview, although both Cornell and Gerards will be free to jump in with follow-up questions.

Gerards, who investigated Susan Smith's disappearance before the FBI joined in, has long been suspicious of Mark Putnam. Pearson remains skeptical. He thinks Mark might shed some new light on the case but doesn't expect much more beyond that.

When the special agent in charge of the Miami office, Graham Blevins, walks in with Mark, Pearson rises from his seat, putting his thoughts aside. He shakes Mark's hand. The young man has a firm grip.

"Thanks for agreeing to meet with us," Pearson says.

"No problem," Mark says. "Whatever I can do to help."

Pearson thinks Mark looks a little concerned but figures that's to be expected. It's not every day that agents from one FBI office come to another to conduct a criminal investigation. But Mark has expressed a willingness—even an eagerness—to help with the case. He declined to have a lawyer present.

"Mark, we've run into some dead ends while looking for this missing informant," Pearson says. "It seems like you knew her pretty well, and we're just hoping there's something you know that might open some new avenues for us."

"Of course," Mark says, sitting up straight with his hands resting casually in his lap.

"Tell us a little about Susan and how you met her."

Mark describes their introduction and how crucial Susan was to the FBI's arrest of Paul Collins, aka Cat Eyes, for a series of bank robberies that had plagued the area.

"How old is Susan?" Pearson asks, flipping through his notes.

"She was twenty-eight," Mark says.

It's a small comment, but Pearson feels the atmosphere in the room change. He doesn't let on that anything has happened, doesn't glance at Jack Cornell or Steven Gerards, doesn't miss a beat as he jumps to his next question.

But he noticed. And he's sure the others did too.

Mark Putnam used the past tense: *She was twenty-eight.*

CHAPTER 33

Washington, DC. Twenty-Four Hours Later

MARK PUTNAM SITS IN the chair trying not to feel anxious as the polygraph technician hooks him up to the machine. There's one sensor monitoring his breathing, another for his pulse, a third for his blood pressure, and finally one to check his perspiration. Mark tries to will himself to relax. He wants to close his eyes and take a deep breath, but he doesn't want to appear concerned about anything.

Pete Pearson stands nearby, observing. When the test begins, he'll leave the room, but for now, he's making sure neither Mark nor the technician need anything. Pearson sat next to Mark on the airplane up here this morning, and the two of them chatted about who had the best chance in the NBA playoffs and whether this would finally be the year Michael Jordan got a ring. But it had been a strained conversation. Neither of them wanted to talk about the case, but they also didn't want to just sit in silence, ignoring each other.

After Mark was questioned for six hours yesterday, Pearson asked if he'd be willing to take a polygraph test. Mark knew they all now suspected him of being involved in Susan's disappearance, but he didn't know how to decline the polygraph without looking guilty.

Instead of arranging a polygraph in Miami, Pearson said they would fly him up to the headquarters in Washington, DC.

"We'll make sure it gets done right," he said. "We'll clear all this up."

He said this matter-of-factly, but they wouldn't be flying all the way to headquarters if the agency wasn't taking this very seriously. A polygraph test would be inadmissible in court, but Mark knows that if the results suggest he is being deceptive, they'll keep investigating him until they find evidence. If he passes the test, they'll finally leave him alone.

"We're ready," says the technician.

As Pearson leaves the room, the technician positions himself behind his machine, which fits inside a briefcase. From where he sits, Mark can't see the needles scrolling out results on the moving paper.

The technician starts with typical yes-or-no questions to establish baseline readings.

"Is your name Mark Putnam?"

"Are you married?"

"Do you live in Florida?"

"Do you work for the FBI?"

But once he's through those, the technician gets straight to the point.

"Did you have a sexual relationship with Susan Smith?" he asks, his voice monotone.

"No," Mark says, trying to believe his own answer.

"Did you have a role in her disappearance?"

"No."

"Did you kill her?"

"No."

The technician looks at his monitor, his expression blank. "Excuse me for a moment," he says. "We'll take a short break."

Without further explanation, the man leaves the room. Less than a minute later, Pete Pearson walks back in.

"Mark, can I talk to you for a second?"

"Sure."

The technician disconnects the cables, freeing Mark to step into the hallway with Pearson.

"I think you know there's a problem with your test," the agent says.

Mark hangs his head, unable to look at his superior.

Pearson's tone is firm but not adversarial; he sounds like a father advising his son that it's time to come clean. "Will you tell us the truth?"

Mark raises his head to look at Pearson. "I need to talk to my wife."

CHAPTER 34

KATHY IS A NERVOUS wreck. She doesn't have the focus to take the kids to story time at the library or to the swimming pool in their condominium complex. She parks them in front of the TV with *Sesame Street* on, and when that's over, she puts in a Disney video.

Until today, she hadn't been worried about any of this business with the Susan Smith investigation. Her concerns started this morning when she walked Mark to the door before he left for the airport. He looked like he hadn't slept. His face looked positively gaunt. *My God,* she thought. *How much weight has he lost?* "Try not to worry," she told him. "Won't it screw up the results if you're stressed?"

"I need to warn you," he said, "this might not go well for me."

Kathy straightened his tie and looked him in the eye

with complete confidence. "You can do this," she said. "You've got nothing to hide."

She'd felt certain this would all be over by nightfall, but after Mark left, she started to feel a growing dread. His nervousness had been contagious. It took her a while to realize what was bothering her, but then it hit her like a thunderclap.

Mark had an affair with Susan.

She suddenly knew it with complete certainty. *How could I not have seen it before?*

Clearly, whatever he had with Susan wasn't serious, Kathy tells herself. *I was miserable and probably insufferable to be around when we lived in Pikeville. Mark was completely stressed out. We never had time alone. We rarely had sex. So what if he screwed around a little when things were tough? But we've made it to the other side of that black period.*

Together.

With Pikeville behind them, Kathy believed their marriage was stronger than ever. They were finally on track to have the life they'd always wanted.

The problem was that if the FBI found out that Mark had an inappropriate relationship with Susan, his career would be over. He would never work in law enforcement again.

When the phone rings, Kathy snatches it from its cradle.

"It's me," Mark says, his voice hollow.

"What's wrong?" Kathy says, not bothering with small talk.

"I've got a problem here in Washington," he says. "I don't know what to do."

"Come back to Florida," Kathy says, panic filling her heart. "We'll get a lawyer. Don't say another word to the FBI without a lawyer."

"I want to get this off my chest," Mark says. "I can't live with the guilt anymore."

"Not this way," she says. "Come back to Florida and tell me here. Then we'll figure this out together. We're a team, remember?"

After Mark hangs up, Kathy is slow to put the phone back in its cradle. She stares out the window at the palm trees swaying in the summer breeze.

I want to get this off my chest, Mark said. *I can't live with the guilt anymore.*

He sounded like someone who wanted to confess to more than an affair.

CHAPTER 35

Three Weeks Later

MARK SITS IN THE conference room at the office of his lawyer, Dominic Newman. Kathy isn't here. She's been alternating between fits of crying, hugging him close, and shouting at him. But so far she hasn't asked for a divorce, which Mark sees as a good sign.

When Pete Pearson arrives at the lawyer's office, he has another agent with him as well as a stenographer.

"I just want to say," Mark begins after the five of them sit down around a large white table, "that I'm sincerely sorry for the shame I've brought to the FBI. I loved working for the FBI, and the last thing I wanted to do was taint its image in the eyes of the public."

"Thanks for saying that, Mark," Pearson says, and he encourages him to begin his story. "I'll stop you with questions if I have any, but I thought I'd just let you start by telling it the way you want to."

Mark takes a deep breath.

For the past two weeks, his lawyer and the commonwealth attorney in Pikeville, Adam Raymond, have been negotiating. The Pikeville judge will have to abide by the attorney's recommendation. If the judge doesn't, everything Mark says today will be inadmissible.

Mark's lawyer was against this. He knows the FBI has no case. He urged Mark not to say anything, to roll the dice and let the FBI try to take it to trial.

Kathy agreed with the lawyer. "Think of the kids," she said. "They need their father."

But Mark is consumed by guilt. He knows he'll go to prison, but maybe there he'll be able to live with himself again.

He doesn't know where to begin. He thinks of the mischievous smile Susan flashed him when they met, of how he was drawn to her personality from the moment they first spoke. He remembers her massaging his shoulders and the way he'd taken comfort in her touch.

How can he explain what happened when he can hardly believe it himself?

I have to say it, he thinks. *I can't hold this inside anymore.*

"I had an affair with Susan Smith," he tells them. "And I killed her."

As he says it, Mark feels a physical relief, as if the burden that's weighed on him is finally easing.

Mark tells the whole story, beginning with when he

met Susan and not stopping until he's described pulling her body out of the trunk and tossing it down the embankment next to the old coal-mine road.

"She accused me of treating her like a piece of meat I could just throw away," he says. "In the end, that's exactly what I did."

When he finishes speaking, Mark puts his head in his hands and sobs.

"I wish I'd come forward sooner," Mark says, wiping his tears with a tissue his lawyer hands him. "I just couldn't bring myself to admit it. I think I always knew I'd get caught and everything would come out. I think I *wanted* it to come out. When I reported her missing, maybe a part of me thought I was covering my tracks. But another part of me wanted someone to find her—so they could find *me*."

CHAPTER 36

AN HOUR LATER, IN the fading glow of sunset, with police lights flashing around them, Detective Steven Gerards and a team of police officers and FBI agents stand at the top of the embankment where Mark Putnam claimed he'd left Susan Smith's body. The ravine is overgrown with thorns and brush. On the other side of the gulch are mounds of rock, piled there back when this part of the mine was operational.

"Let's get started," Gerards says. "Fan out."

The men descend, spaced out in order to cover the maximum area. It's only a matter of minutes before someone calls out, "Over here!"

Gerards fights his way through the thicket and comes to where the trooper is standing.

A skeleton lies in the gravel. Some of the bones are scattered—perhaps torn away from the body by animals—but for the most part, the skeleton remains intact. The bones seem tiny to Gerards; he hadn't realized just how petite Susan was. He thinks of how strong and athletic Mark Putnam looks.

You poor girl, he thinks. *You never stood a chance against him.*

There are no signs that Susan was wearing any clothes, but tangled in the vertebrae of her neck is a small gold chain with a tiny cross, glinting in the last light of sunset.

Gerards climbs up the embankment as the forensic team begins collecting the bones. Standing on the edge of the road, police lights flashing around him, the detective is lost in thought. He's been looking for Susan Smith since Mark Putnam first called the state police to report her missing, but finding her—what was left of her—this way doesn't feel like anything to be proud of.

When Pearson called to tell him the location of the body, he also quickly summarized how Putnam said he'd killed her. But Gerards is not satisfied with Mark Putnam's version of the story, and his mind is full of lingering questions. Was it really a crime of passion? Or was it premeditated? Did he invite her to go for a drive, knowing he would kill her?

And even if it was a crime of passion—even if Putnam let his anger get the best of him for a moment—what kind of unhinged psychopath drives around with a body in his trunk, letting the car sit at a parking meter while he's at work?

Gerards knows he'll have to let go of these questions and learn to live with the outcome of the case. Susan Smith didn't live to tell her side of the story. Mark Putnam said he just wanted to shut her up.

It worked.

He silenced her forever.

As Gerards prepares to head back into town to call Pearson in Miami with an update, a coal truck rolls down the road and slows as it approaches the flashing lights. It pulls to a stop and the driver leans out of the open window.

"What y'all doing?" he asks.

"We're recovering a body," Gerards says. "Homicide investigation."

"Good timing," the trucker says.

"What do you mean?"

"See all that rock?" the man says, gesturing to the mounds of gravel on the other side of the ravine. "We were planning to bulldoze all that into the gulch tomorrow. Another twenty-four hours and whatever is down there would have been buried beneath fifty feet of rock."

CHAPTER 37

Pikeville, Kentucky. June 1990

MOLLY DAVIDSON APPROACHES THE court-house in Pikeville on the morning Mark Putnam is scheduled to appear for his hearing. She walks with purpose, her handbag slung over her shoulder, here to represent her kid sister Susan.

As she approaches the newspaper reporters cluster-ing around the door, Molly hears one of them say, "That's the sister," and suddenly they converge on her, throwing out questions.

"Molly," one of them says, "are you satisfied with the sentence the commonwealth attorney is recom-mending?"

The attorneys had put forth a charge of manslaughter, not murder, and were recommending sixteen years in a federal prison, not a state prison. Mark would be eligible for parole in a decade.

"Absolutely not," Molly says, raising her head high

and preparing to get off her chest all the thoughts that have been building up inside her. "Mark Putnam could be out of prison in ten years, but my sister is dead forever. Where is the justice in that?"

"Have you talked to Adam Raymond about why he took the deal?" one of the reporters asks.

Molly isn't the only one who's been critical of the authorities. Newspapers in the tri-corner region had been lambasting the FBI, the commonwealth attorney's office, and the state police for bungling the investigation and prosecution. Molly understands that some of this criticism isn't warranted. Detective Steven Gerards took her concerns seriously from the start, and commonwealth attorney Adam Raymond didn't have much choice—it was either make a deal or risk letting Mark Putnam walk.

But Molly believes the FBI deserves all of the criticism it's received—and more.

"I understand the commonwealth attorney's hands were tied," Molly continues, "but the FBI sat on their hands for almost a year after my sister went missing. They're all proud of themselves for solving this case within weeks of getting involved. But she went missing June of last year. They used Susan as an informant and then when it was obvious to anyone who would look that one of their agents had something to do with her disappearance, they turned their heads the other way and acted like they had no responsibility.

"I know what they're going to say in court today," she says. "They're going to paint the picture of Mark Putnam as some kind of victim here. 'He's a good guy who just made a mistake. Poor pitiful Mark Putnam, with his prep-school education and his athletic scholarship and his fancy FBI badge—if only that hillbilly girl hadn't thrown herself at him, he might have had a bright future.'

"Mark Putnam is not the victim—my sister is the victim. He recruited her to work for the FBI. He got her to do his bidding. He had power over her. It was his responsibility to keep the relationship professional. She trusted him, and he repaid that trust by strangling her to death and going to work the next morning with her body in his trunk.

"All this just sends a message to the world what the federal government thinks about us. If you want to get away with murder, just make sure you come to Kentucky to do it—and make sure your victim is poor and female."

As the journalists scratch frantically on their notepads, Molly says that if they have any more questions, she'll answer them after the hearing.

"If you'll excuse me," she says, "I want to go inside now and get a good seat. If I get the chance, I'm going to spit in Mark Putnam's face."

This last statement gets a few nervous laughs from the journalists, who don't know if she's joking.

Molly enters the courthouse and joins the queue to go through security. She drops her handbag on the conveyor belt and steps through the checkpoint. She waits for her purse to come out of the x-ray machine. Before she can grab it off the conveyor belt, one of the deputies says, "Wait a minute."

He snatches the bag and unzips it. Tucked into an inside pocket is the snub-nosed .38 she always carries in the bag.

"Oh, hell," she says. "I forgot that was in there."

The security guard stares at her.

"Ma'am," he says, "you're under arrest."

CHAPTER 38

KATHY PUTNAM SITS AT home, waiting to hear from Mark's lawyer, Dominic Newman, who'd told her that Mark would be able to call her after the hearing, before he was taken to prison.

Kathy can't stop crying.

Her parents, who flew down from Connecticut to help, have taken the kids to the pool so that she can be alone when Mark calls. As she waits, Kathy tries to calm her nerves by pouring herself a glass of vodka and soda. She chose vodka when she was at the liquor store yesterday so that the kids—and her parents— wouldn't smell alcohol on her breath.

As she takes a large swallow, she thinks of Susan and how obvious it had been that she was smitten with Mark. But Kathy would never have befriended her if she'd understood the threat Susan posed to her marriage. She could have steered Mark away from her.

She could have warned him that Susan would try to worm her way into his life.

Part of her knows it's wrong to blame Susan. Whatever mistakes the woman made, she didn't deserve to pay with her life. When Mark told her what he'd done, initially Kathy had been in shock. Then she'd been angry with him. In the days after he told her, she'd debated what to do, ultimately concluding that she wouldn't let a mistake—even one this big—tear them apart. Mark had known about Kathy's own past mistakes, yet he had still stood with her on the altar and vowed to love her for better or worse.

Now it's her turn to stand with him.

As soon as the phone rings, Kathy snatches it up. "Are you okay? What happened?"

"Everything went as expected," Mark says with resignation. "I can't talk long. We're heading to the airport soon. I can't believe I'm going to prison."

He tells her that it feels weird to wear handcuffs. He'd put cuffs on other people but had never known what they felt like on his own wrists. Kathy's heart breaks when she thinks of her husband, the FBI agent, now handcuffed like a criminal.

Not *like* a criminal. He *is* a criminal.

As she starts to cry, he says, for what must be the hundredth time since he broke the news to her about killing Susan, that he's sorry. "I love you."

"I love you too," she says. "I'll wait for you. *We'll*

wait for you. This isn't the end for our family. We'll be happy again."

But after she hangs up the phone, she sobs into her hands. Then pours herself another drink.

She doesn't know how she'll ever be happy again.

EPILOGUE

Summer 1998. Eight Years Later

MOLLY DAVIDSON WALKS THE cracked paved path through the cemetery to her sister's grave. She places a bunch of flowers—begonias, petunias, and zinnias picked from her own garden—on the overgrown grass. Susan's headstone is a simple bronze marker, paid for by the state of Kentucky. Six feet below, her sister's bones lie in a child-size casket.

There had been no need for an adult-size coffin. There wasn't enough left of Susan to fill it.

Molly stands sweating in the summer heat. It's late in the afternoon and there isn't any shade next to Susan's grave. The sky is the color of faded denim, and the humidity is oppressive.

Molly tries to make this trip at least once a month. She comes and tells her sister—if there's anything left of her spirit in this world or in heaven—about all that's going on in the family. How Samantha and Alex are doing, how they're growing like weeds, that she'd be amazed at how tall they've become. She tells Susan about her brothers and sisters, nieces and nephews.

In the past, she'd also updated Susan about developments in the case related to Mark Putnam, but there hasn't been anything new in that area for a few years.

While the gun charges were looming over her, Molly had refrained from publicly criticizing the Kentucky law enforcement agencies who investigated her sister's death and prosecuted the murderer. But once the charges were dropped, Molly continued fighting for some semblance of justice for her sister.

Molly decried the FBI in the newspapers and filed a lawsuit against the agency, hoping to raise money for Susan's children. But the suit was thrown out for technical reasons she didn't understand.

Apparently, the FBI briefly suspended a couple of people—Mark's partner Glen Bell and his supervisor Trent Cavanagh—but otherwise, the agency quickly washed its hands of the whole mess and did not take any responsibility for how it had mismanaged its informants, failed to supervise its agent, and looked the other way when it was obvious one of its agents had something to do with Susan's disappearance.

Molly had also sued Mark Putnam, but even though the judge awarded her almost a million dollars in damages, the son of a bitch declared bankruptcy, and her family never got a cent.

That left Susan's kids without a mother and still as poor as ever.

Molly prayed for them every night and asked Susan to watch over them from heaven if she could.

Today, however, Molly is here with different news.

"I came to tell you," Molly says, swallowing hard, "about Kathy."

A few years after Susan was buried and after the lawsuits had all amounted to nothing, Molly had decided to write Kathy Putnam a letter. She felt Mark's wife was also a victim of his. He'd killed Susan, and he'd destroyed Kathy's life too.

To Molly's surprise, Kathy wrote her back. They exchanged letters for a while and then began talking on the phone.

Kathy was easy to talk to; Molly could see why her sister had spent so many hours on the phone with her. And Molly suspected that she somehow filled the void of friendship that Susan's death had left.

Molly knew it was an unconventional friendship that nobody else understood, but she and Kathy had bonded over the tragedy of Susan's death.

They were both collateral damage.

Molly knew that Mark had bounced around various federal prisons over the past eight years, some of them essentially country clubs, with tennis courts, swimming pools, and restaurant-quality food. Now he was in Massachusetts and probably had only a couple of years left before he was released. He might be a little grayer, his body a little heavier, but he'd still be alive and well when he got out. Mostly Kathy remained mum about her continued devotion to him, and somehow the two women ignored the fact that Molly hated—despised— the man that Kathy loved.

Somehow their friendship worked.

They were united in sorrow, even if they weren't mourning the same thing.

On these graveside visits, Molly also often updated Susan about Kathy and her kids. She thought her sister would want to know. But today, she has something difficult to say.

"Kathy died," Molly tells her, choking back tears.

Earlier this morning when the phone rang, Molly had wondered if it might be Kathy, since she hadn't heard from her in a few weeks. To Molly's surprise, however, it was Jenny, Kathy's daughter.

"I thought you should know that Mom's dead," the little girl said, sounding older than her thirteen years. "She would have wanted me to call you."

Jenny explained that she'd come home from school to find her mom on the couch, unmoving. Molly knew that Kathy had become a heavy drinker after Mark's arrest, and it was a regular occurrence for her children to get back from school and find their mom passed out.

But that day, when Jenny tried to rouse her mother, she found her body cold and stiff.

The doctors determined that the cause of death was heart failure, but Kathy was only thirty-eight years old. She'd been depressed and consuming alcohol at an alarming rate over the years since Mark had been incarcerated.

The bottom line was, she drank herself to death.

Kathy had stood by her husband through everything, but the position he'd put her in had been too much to bear. He'd murdered Susan, but, indirectly, he'd killed Kathy too. Molly can't help but reflect on how unfair it is that he'll soon be free while both of the women caught in his love triangle are now dead.

Molly kneels in the grass in front of Susan's grave as she tells all this to the empty air. She stares at the cross embossed on the bronze grave marker and remembers the small cross Susan used to wear around her neck.

Maybe Mark Putnam really did feel guilty for what he'd done, as he claimed in his confession, and maybe he'd become a better person while in prison. Reform was possible, of course.

But as Molly rises from the grave and walks back to her car, she thinks that she may never be able to let go of her anger at Mark Putnam for causing so much destruction to so many lives. If it had been the other way around and Susan had somehow killed *him* in a fit of rage, she would have spent the rest of her life behind bars. She might have been given the death penalty.

But he'll spend only ten years in prison.

Molly can imagine him now, walking out of prison, hugging his kids. Taking a breath of fresh air. Getting to start over.

A second chance.

Which was more than Susan ever got.

ABOUT THE AUTHORS

James Patterson is the world's bestselling author and most trusted storyteller. He has created many enduring fictional characters and series, including Alex Cross, the Women's Murder Club, Michael Bennett, Maximum Ride, Middle School, and I Funny. Among his notable literary collaborations are *The President Is Missing*, with President Bill Clinton, and the Max Einstein series, produced in partnership with the Albert Einstein Estate. Patterson's writing career is characterized by a single mission: to prove that there is no such thing as a person who "doesn't like to read," only people who haven't found the right book. He's given over three million books to schoolkids and the military, donated more than seventy million dollars to support education, and endowed over five thousand college scholarships for teachers. For his prodigious imagination and championship of literacy in America, Patterson was awarded the 2019 National Humanities Medal. The National

Book Foundation presented him with the Literarian Award for Outstanding Service to the American Literary Community, and he is also the recipient of an Edgar Award and nine Emmy Awards. He lives in Florida with his family.

Andrew Bourelle is the author of the novel *Heavy Metal* and coauthor with James Patterson of *Texas Ranger*. His short stories have been published widely in literary magazines and fiction anthologies, including *The Best American Mystery Stories*.

Max DiLallo is a novelist, playwright, and screenwriter. He lives in Los Angeles.

For a complete list of books by

JAMES PATTERSON

VISIT
JamesPatterson.com

 Follow James Patterson on Facebook
@JamesPatterson

 Follow James Patterson on Twitter
@JP_Books

 Follow James Patterson on Instagram
@jamespattersonbooks